How To Buy
YOUR FIRST HOME

How To Buy
YOUR FIRST HOME
Without Any Snags

Be one of the millions to do so!!!

Are you renting? …

Are myths of home ownership stopping you? …

Are you letting past events hold you back? …

Take the FEAR out of owning a HOME now! …

Dr. Mark L. Huddleston Ph.D

XULON PRESS

Xulon Press
555 Winderley Pl, Suite 225
Maitland, FL 32751
407.339.4217
www.xulonpress.com

Paperback ISBN-13: 978-1-66288-757-4
Ebook ISBN-13: 978-1-66288-758-1

Inspiring Quotes

We are our worst enemies. We build invisible barriers around ourselves and go into battle, already defeated and conquered. We live only to exist and die hopelessly in those self-made prisons we have created for ourselves... *Dr. Mark L. Huddleston Ph.D., DCC, CFA, CLC.*

When will it ever be the right time? If not first, you take the time to make some time...? *Dr. Mark L. Huddleston Ph.D., DCC, CFA, CLC.*

It takes change for change to take place... *Dr. Mark L. Huddleston Ph.D., DCC, CFA, CLC.*

Pain is inevitable; being miserable is by choice...*Dr. Mark L. Huddleston, Ph.D., DCC, CFA, CLC.*

Every problem contains the solution within itself...*Dr. Mark L. Huddleston Ph.D., DCC, CFA, CLC.*

We must motivate, inspire, and encourage at every given opportunity... *God.*

To get something you never had, you must do something you never did......*Unknown.*

The more you know, the less you need to say... *Unknown.*

To know health is to be healthy...*Dr. Mark L. Huddleston, Ph.D., DCC, CFA, CLC.*

Instead of worrying about things you can't change, start thinking about things you can change... *Dr. Mark L. Huddleston Ph.D., DCC, CFA, CLC.*

Anything that happens in your life, may it be good or bad, is a direct result of something you did, did not do, should have done, or shouldn't have done. You must learn to take credit as well as the blame when it comes to your life... *Dr. Mark L. Huddleston Ph.D., DCC, CFA, CLC.*

The battle between good and evil, production and destruction, is first fought in the mind and must be won on the battleground of the mind... *Dr. Mark L. Huddleston Ph.D. DCC, CFA, CLC.*

Ignorance breeds unawareness; knowledge breeds greatness...*Dr. Mark L. Huddleston Ph.D. DCC, CFA, CLC.*

Why ask how a person can do so many things when you should be asking yourself why you can't ... *Dr. Mark L. Huddleston Ph.D., DCC, CFA, CLC.*

They say to know love is to have felt love and to have squandered it away... *Dr. Mark L. Huddleston Ph.D., DCC, CFA, CLC.*

Admitting that we are wrong is the first step of making it right... *Dr. Mark L. Huddleston Ph.D., DCC, CFA, CLC.*

Greatness does not come easy; it must be desired first, sought after, and earned if it is to be achieved... *Dr. Mark L. Huddleston Ph.D., DCC, CFA, CLC.*

If you cannot do great things, do small things in a significant way ... *Napoleon Hill*

If you continue to do what you have always done, you will continue to be what you have always been... *Unknown.*

Destiny is not a matter of chance but a matter of choice ... *Unknown.*

You should stop living in fear of living... *Dr. Mark L. Huddleston Ph.D., DCC, CFA, CLC.*

I would rather take the hand of someone that has done it already than take the hand of a fool that has no clue... *Dr. Mark L. Huddleston Ph.D., DCC, CFA, CLC.*

Without change in yourself, there can be no change in your life... *Dr. Mark L. Huddleston Ph.D., DCC, CFA, CLC.*

A negative mind will never produce a positive life... *Dr. Mark L. Huddleston Ph.D., DCC, CFA, CLC.*

You should always dress for the job you want, not the job you have. Just as you can choose to live the life you want to live

rather than settling for the one you have and dreaming of a better one... *Unknown*

Most of us choose the opposite path that was chosen for us. We would rather climb a seamless mountain than accept a helicopter ride to the top ... *Dr. Mark L. Huddleston Ph.D., DCC, CFA, CLC.*

If you are looking for guarantees, one thing is for sure. If you do nothing, nothing is guaranteed to happen, but if you do something, you have guaranteed yourself the opportunity of making something happen ... *Dr. Mark L. Huddleston Ph.D., DCC, CFA, CLC.*

You should learn how to get out of your own way, for in most cases, you are the sole cause of your failures as well as your successes ... *Dr. Mark L. Huddleston Ph.D., DCC, CFA, CLC.*

You don't stop progressing because you grow old. You grow old because you stop progressing ... *Dr. Mark L. Huddleston Ph.D., DCC, CFA, CLC.*

Everyone is in a rush to go nowhere and a bigger rush to do nothing once they get there ... *Dr. Mark L. Huddleston Ph.D., DCC, CFA, CLC.*

I find it fascinating that most people can come up with all kinds of excuses why they can't do something and no reasons or justifications of how they can do something ... *Dr. Mark L. Huddleston Ph.D., DCC, CFA, CLC.*

Your children are a product of your thinking ... *Dr. Mark L. Huddleston Ph.D., DCC, CFA, CLC.*

Become the thought that you want to become ... *Dr. Mark L. Huddleston Ph.D., DCC, CFA, CLC.*

Pick up other books that Dr. Huddleston has written.

"The Manufacturing Of A Dream"

"The Rewards Of Healing A Broken Body The Alternative Way"

"Building And Maintaining A Strong And Everlasting Relationship"

"Eluding The Toxic Enemy Within"

"The Essential Keys To Financial Freedom"

"Principles of Achievement"

"How To Get Employers To Call YOU When Seeking The JOB You Want"

DISCLAIMER

The information provided in this publication does not, and is not intended to, constitute legal advice and should not be relied upon in lieu of consultation with appropriate legal advisers in the appropriate jurisdiction.

This book should not be a substitute for direct, personalized, and relevant advice from an attorney, financial adviser, real estate agent, or escrow/closing agent. Although the author and publisher have made every effort to ensure that the information in this book is correct and accurate, the author and publisher do not assume and hereby disclaim any liability to party for any loss, damage, or disruption caused by errors or omissions, whether such errors or omissions result from negligence, accident, or any other cause.

The publisher and author are not responsible for any real estate or financial transaction undertaken by the reader. Purchasing this book does not create a fiduciary or professional relationship with the publisher or author. The publication may not entirely capture current laws and practices as the subject matter changes frequently and is subject to wide variability among jurisdictions.

Please consult with a licensed attorney or real estate professional regarding any financial or real estate transactions you plan on making.

I stress that this book is for educational purposes only, and you and only you are responsible if you choose to do anything based on what you have read.

If you are unwilling to comply with these limitations, we ask that you do **NOT** read this publication...

-Dr. Mark L. Huddleston Ph.D., DCC, CFA. CLC.

Dedication

I would like to dedicate this book to my family and everyone I know and have come in contact with throughout my life; they have all given me strength and the reason to work harder and to be more creative in everything I do.

I would also like to dedicate this book to God Almighty! After accepting Jesus as my Lord and Savior, I have learned to walk by faith and not by sight. I am now RICH IN FAITH! Oh Lord, YOU are my everything! Without YOU in my life, I would be nothing! To God, be the Glory! AMEN.

-Dr. Mark L. Huddleston Ph.D., DCC, CFA, CLC.

TABLE OF CONTENTS

Thoughts of the Author

We live in different times than our parents did when they were our age. The need for inspiration, motivation, and encouragement is at an all-time high.

According to recently conducted surveys in the United States, Americans face severe all-around difficulties. Many people I have spoken to are scared about their future.

Many people live under the misconception that ordinary people like you and I can't become millionaires or live comfortable everyday lives like the elite 5% of the world. The reason most of us feel this way is due to being mentally conditioned from childhood that only "**those people**" can live a lifestyle that we all at one time dreamed of.

The truth is that when we were children, we used to dream of doing big things, becoming doctors, astronauts, basketball players, presidents, and teachers. The Sky was the limit. There were no boundaries to what we could or could not accomplish. We set the tone and the outcome of every dream we ever dreamed of when we were young. Our thoughts were endless. So, what happened?

Let me tell you what happened. Somewhere in time, a person we respected very much told us that we were crazy and that dreaming was foolish, and we believed them. They told us that dreaming was for the mentally ill. That we needed to live in reality, the here and now, and that only "**those people**" were allowed to dream and live the good life.

I always wondered what made "**those people**" better than me. "**Those people**" looked like me. They acted like me. They wore the same clothes as me. They eat the same food as me. They were no smarter than me. They were no faster or stronger than I was. So why was I not allowed to be like "**those people**." Was there a law that I didn't know about? And if there was such a law, who was enforcing it? Why was I not chosen to be one of "**those people?**"

Let me be the first to tell you that all of us who choose to can become one of "**those people**." Throughout this book, I will cover many principles and disciplines that, if implemented and applied daily, not only will your life exponentially change, but it will also have far more positive implications than you ever thought possible.

You must understand that the number one reason for the disparity in one's life is due solely to procrastination and ignorance. Your height, skin color, race, or nationality has nothing to do with consistency and discipline in your life. Now that the cat is out of the bag and there are no more excuses you can use, let's move in a more productive direction to obtain a beneficial outcome. The home and life you **want** are waiting for you to claim them! So, let's get started and make it happen **NOW!**

FOREWORD

Right now, people are frightened about their future. They want to stay expanded in a world that is contracting. People wonder how they can evolve when the world is dissolving right in front of them. Some of you may have questions like, how can I make it through the month? How can I grow in prosperity? How can I achieve a sense of well-being and harmony in my life?

Something within you knows that there are answers to those profound questions waiting for you to discover them. Something within you knows that there is greatness within you, trying to emanate from you. You will find that you have gifts that have been bestowed on you by the Creator of all things. You are an avenue of consciousness that only needs fine tweaking to perform optimally.

Everyone reading this book has what it takes to be more than what they are now. There are no new secrets out there that will expedite your greatness. Only applying the principles laid out in this book will help you discover your innate gifts and their importance to you. Once you become more conscious of these innate gifts, the more you will become enlightened about how these gifts can benefit you and everyone linked to you.

Once you understand what these innate gifts can do for you, you will no longer have to be a victim of the past. You will no longer have to be a victim of circumstance. You will no longer have to think about lack or worry. You will never have to fall victim to anything negative ever again. You will know without a doubt that those innate gifts are within you, just waiting to sustain you from all negativity that may come your way. You will no longer feel that prosperity is right outside your grasp.

You will come to know that you have been given the number one gift ever given to any creature or human being on planet earth. That gift would be the power to **choose**. You have the potential to be what you want to be. If you **choose** to be happy, you can be happy. If you **choose** to be sad, you can be sad. If you **choose** to be rich, you can be rich. If you **choose** to own a home, you can own a home. The choice is yours.

I know what you're thinking. It sounds too simple to be true. That's the problem with the world today. If something is simple, we go out of our way to make it difficult. We can't seem to leave well enough alone. Don't become one of those who conform and follow the follower. **Choose** to think outside the box. **Choose** to be all that you can be. But first, you have to practice and apply these principles daily and believe they will work for you.

CHAPTER ONE

THE IMPORTANCE OF KNOWING WHO YOU ARE AND WHAT YOU WANT OUT OF LIFE

When will it ever be the right time?
If not first you take the time to make some time.
-Dr. Mark L. Huddleston PhD

I t is my opinion that if you want to elude the toxic enemy within yourself, you must **first** <u>find out who you are</u>, and **secondly**, you must <u>find out what you want out of life</u>. I know it sounds simple, but 95% of us will never know these two things before we cease to exist.

I want to point out that you are your worst enemy in life. No one does more harm to you than you. Now that you know who your greatest adversary is, you can learn to defend yourself against yourself.

Have you noticed that very few people ever reach for the stars while they are living? Only in death will those people ever get there. I was told a story long ago that went something like this. All the stars you see in the sky are unfulfilled dreams of every person that was ever born. When you see a falling star, it represents a dream that has come true. The moral of this story is simple; most of us have dreams that go unfulfilled, with only a few of us ever seeing our dreams come to pass.

The reason for this is due to the company we keep and a weak belief system in place. Just think back to when you were a baby. You crawled around on all fours exploring your surroundings without any fear whatsoever. You were adventurous and courageous. You were persistent at trying to talk and to walk. If you fell down, you did not hesitate to try to get back up again. When you learned how to put sounds together, you did not stop until you were able to utter words that became familiar to you.

Do you see where I am going with this? From the day you were born, everyone that surrounded you was pushing you to become a better you. No one was hindering your personal growth and development. It was all right for you to take chances and to live life on the edge. The people who had a hand in raising you exposed you to many things and aided you in expanding your mental capacity.

If you cannot think back to your childhood, you might want to talk to your parents or people involved in your upbringing and ask them what type of baby you were. You may find out a lot about who you are. I have to warn you that you may be disappointed with what you find out. You may find yourself asking what happened to that adventurous and courageous spirit you once had. Why don't you still possess these exceptional qualities?

The truth of the matter is that someone very important and close to you told you that it was not okay to dream or reach for the stars. When that person told you that it was not okay to be you, your whole world collapsed, and your spirit was devastated and shattered. Not many people ever recover from a broken spirit.

Someone whom I respected and thought was close to me broke my spirit many times. There were many times I thought of taking my own life due to the mental punishment I endured by this person. After a while, I could not be in the same room with that person without feeling nauseous and sickly. After a while, I had put two and two together and knew that it was that person that was making me feel the way that I was feeling. I knew that this person was sucking the life out of me, and if I did not get as far away from that person as possible, I knew I would either take my own life or take theirs. Taking my life was not an option, so I moved on and never looked back. I never regretted making that move, and now that I think about it, I feel it was the best thing that I ever did in my life.

After making that move, I began to recover from the mental beatings that I endured at the hands of that person. As time passed, my spirit began to heal once again. I started to feel good about myself. I began to dream again. I began to love who I was and how I was feeling. I was no longer ashamed of my dreams and aspirations. I took the time to learn about myself.

Moving away from the toxic influences in my life, I began to deal with the toxic enemy within myself. I knew deep down inside that there were things I wanted to achieve and accomplish in my life. I knew that my purpose in life was much more than being a human punching bag for everyone around me to use at their leisure.

Once I figured out that I was not going to die by distancing myself from the negative influences in my life, I was now able to concentrate on finding out who I was and what I was made of. I wrote down my likes and dislikes. I made sure I was true to myself when doing so. Most of the time, you are not true to yourself; you don't stand behind your beliefs, views, and philosophies. You deviate from the **TRUTH** of how you feel due to peer pressure or plain cowardice. Either way, you are not allowing yourself to pursue your true calling or purpose in life. This is what is called **SELF-HUMILIATION!**

The secret to finding out who you truly are and what makes you tick is to be true to yourself at all times. Not allowing anyone or anything the power to deter you from being you. You must never let your guard down at a single moment. You must always remember that you are your worst enemy or your best friend. Only you can decide what side of the truth you will be part of. You can be your best friend or your worst enemy; the choice is yours to make and no one else's.

I must warn you now that it will not be easy learning to live by truth, for you have been living a lie most of your life trying to keep up with the Jones, not knowing that the Jones are living a lie also. You must learn to walk by faith and not by sight, for what you see may not be all that it is made up to be.

Let me reiterate this thought. I am sure you have neighbors that have a big house, 3 to 4 luxury cars in the driveway, wearing six-thousand-dollar suits, wearing $100,000 in jewelry, and giving lavish parties every other weekend. What you don't know is that only 5% of the human population can afford to live this way. Now, if this figure is the truth, that would mean that 95% of the human population is living a lie. This would mean that most of the human population is in debt up to their eyeballs, wondering how they are going to make their next mortgage payment or what bill they are going to put off this month so they can continue to put on their false façade. There are millions of families living this way that are 65 to 90 payments past due on their mortgage, freeloading off the system and everyone else around them.

Don't believe everything you hear. This is one of the number one evils that humanity is faced with today. Most of the information that is being shared on TV and the Internet is not the truth, and most of humanity is not aware of this fact. I have not turned on a TV in the past many years. My conscience was telling me that what I was subjecting myself to was not the truth, and I was not going to allow the government and society the power to dictate who I was going to be or how I was going to think.

I knew that I had the choice to control the information I was absorbing. I knew that if I wanted to know more about myself that I would have to follow my conscience and follow what I believed to be the truth.

Many say that "the grass is greener on the other side of the fence." What those same people don't know is that if they took care of their side of the fence and stopped worrying about the other side of the fence, their side of the fence could look just as good or better.

I guess what I am trying to convey is that you must begin to live the truth, speak the truth, believe the truth, and embrace the truth if you want to truly find out who you are and what you want out of life.

Now that I had found truth in my life, the next thing I had to come to grips with was what type of person I was. I would look into the mirror in my bedroom and ask myself questions that other people had asked me throughout my lifetime. Since I had found truth in my life, I could now answer those questions candidly without the thought of humiliation. Here are some of the questions I would ask myself daily during my self-identifying period.

✓ Am I a good person?
✓ Do I love who I am?
✓ Do I genuinely love other people?
✓ Am I a materialistic person?
✓ Do I live above my means?
✓ Am I a lazy person?
✓ Do I procrastinate?
✓ Do I see things through to the end?
✓ Do I depend on others to get the job done?
✓ Do I invest in myself? (Self-improvement) education, computer, language courses?
✓ Do I let my pride dictate who I am?
✓ Do I lie to myself and others?
✓ Do I want more out of life?
✓ Am I a happy or miserable person?
✓ Am I where I want to be in life?
✓ What things make me happy?
✓ What things upset me?
✓ Do I have a life game plan written down?
✓ Am I adequately protected? Health, income, assets.
✓ Am I debt-free? If not, do I have a plan to get out of debt?
✓ Do I have a retirement plan established?
✓ Do I have a Will and revocable trust set up?
✓ Do I have a list of beneficiaries in case of illness or death?
✓ Do I have a family that I can trust?
✓ Do I have any real friends? If so, what are their names?
✓ Are you meeting new people consistently?
✓ Do you feel you are growing mentally and spiritually?

✓ Are you allowing yourself the opportunity to change and become a better person?
✓ Am I surrounded by positive and supportive people?
✓ Am I surrounded by negative and deleterious people?

These are just some of the questions I used to ask myself every day until I took action on them. Since I now believed in truth, I was able to answer these questions genuinely without embarrassment. I knew that I was in the spirit-rebuilding period of my life. I knew that spirit rebuilding would fall into place as long as I believed in truth and my ability to heal myself from the mental beatings I endured most of my life.

The next thing I did was not allow myself to dwell on the negative events of my life. I knew that if I did, I would relive the events and relive the mental beatings over and over again. I knew I had to let those negative thoughts go if I was to move on with life and get better. Most of us never relinquish control of the negative events we have experienced throughout our lifetime. This is why most of you will never heal and progress in life.

Along with discarding the negative events in your life, you would also have to scrap and thrust aside the negative people in your life. This is easier said than done. Most of you will find this the hardest thing to do in your life. The reason is that you have been programmed since birth that you need to have friends to succeed in life and to have a sense of belonging. The caveat of all of this is that most of you don't have a clue of what a true friend consists of. Most of you think that every person you meet is your friend, and this would be the furthest thing from the truth. The raw reality would be that you may only have one true friend in your lifetime. Don't take me wrong; there are some of you who may have more than one true friend, and that is great, but the fact of the matter is most of you don't.

I don't want to go into great detail about friends right now because I have dedicated a chapter on this subject later on in the book. I will mention that we all have acquaintances, associates, colleagues, and comrades throughout our lifetime, but none of these associations would be considered a friend.

There are two different types of people in this world. You have positive people and negative people. Most of you will never be able to distinguish the difference between the two. And because of this fact, you will never move forward in your life. You will sit idly by and allow the negative people to dictate your every thought and suck your reason for living right out of you. Let's move on!

Knowing what you want out of life

The next thing I would like to share with you is the importance of knowing what you want out of life. You may think this is a simple feat but let me be the first to tell you that it isn't. Once again, I will bring up the figure 5%. This figure represents the portion of people that are (financially independent). 95% is the figure that represents the portion of the people known as the have-nots (not financially independent). The gap between the haves and have-nots is growing at an alarming rate. Once upon a time, there used to be three different social classes that every human being fell under. There were your upper-class people, there were your middle-class people, and there were your lower-class people. At this time, the middle class has deteriorated down to lower class status. You now only have two social classes: the rich and the poor. This is breaking things down into the simplest terms so that everyone can comprehend what is truly going on.

Knowing what you want out of life now and in the future is very important. If you have no clue where you are going, how will you ever get there? Have you ever gone hiking in a remote area that you have never been to before? Did you bring a map, compass, or GPS device? Of course you did. That is how you were able to get back home or get to the place you set out to explore. I am sure you have seen the many news programs showing hikers that have been lost in the mountains for several days without food and water. This is a clear example of foolish people having no clue what they want out of life. They had no clue where they were going and how to get there. They also did not prepare in advance for what things they were going to need before they started their quest.

The reason why I am sharing this story with you is to help change your mindset so that you can comprehend what I am about to educate you about. Knowing what you want will be the driving force behind everything you strive for.

Have you thought about the things you want in life? I mean, have you written down the things you would like to have and accomplish in life? If you have not written down what you want in life and what you want to achieve in life, those thoughts will remain just that, THOUGHTS!

Once your thoughts hit paper, your thoughts become tangible, and they become real. You can now touch your thoughts. You can now share your thoughts with others. You can now begin to construct your thoughts and manufacture your thoughts, just like building a home. Once your thoughts hit paper, it is like pouring the foundation for a new home. You have to start somewhere. Writing your thoughts down would have to be the most important thing when it comes to knowing what you want in life. 95% of you will never write your thoughts down, and that is why 95% of you will never accomplish a thing in your lifetime.

After writing down your thoughts on paper, you will need to figure out everything you are going to need to construct those thoughts. If you don't know everything that you are going to need to construct your thoughts, don't be afraid to ask. This is the next important thing when it comes to knowing what you want in life. If you don't know how to do something, then find a mentor or find someone that knows about whatever it is you are trying to accomplish or construct. Never forget "that a closed mouth never gets fed."

Once you have found the source of your needed data, you will want to have all of your questions written down so that you can present your source with those questions. So many of you don't take the time to write your questions down. When the opportunity presents itself, you are unable to capitalize on the opportunity, or you just shoot from the hip and miss the opportunity altogether. Once again, you can be your worst enemy! Procrastination has held so many of you back and will continue to hold you back until you can lick this bad habit. You must reprogram yourself to act on the moment. It is quite true that the early bird gets the worm, and the second mouse gets the cheese. When acting in the moment, don't be foolish when doing so. Think before you respond, or you may end up like the first mouse.

Finding the gift, ability, or skill deep within you

Did you know that every one of you possesses a gift, ability, or skill that is unique only to you? Let me explain further. Every one of you has some type of ability that you can do or achieve without much effort on your part. Some of you can paint a masterpiece without instruction, education, or tutoring. Some of you can sing like a professional without even thinking about it, and some of you are good with statistics, figures, and equations, and others are good at building things or putting things together. Whatever the gift, ability, or skill, every one of you has one. The hardest trick of all is finding out what it is.

Most of you come upon your special gift, ability, or skill by being exposed to many different things during your childhood, and some of you stumble across your gift, ability, or skill by accident. In other cases, you are never exposed to your gift, ability, or skill, and this is unfortunate.

This does not mean you will never find out what your gift, ability, or skill is; what it does mean is that it will take some work on your part to find out. You may want to pull out your pad and pen and start writing down things that you find interesting or what you are drawn to. Are there things that you are passionate about? Do you find yourself dreaming about certain things all the time? Your dreams can tell you a lot about yourself and what frame of mind you are in. This is why you may have heard so many times in your life from TV shows, teachers, and doctors alike, to follow your dreams.

After making your list of things that interest you, things that you are drawn to, or things you are passionate about, you will then want to meditate over your list and wait to see what jumps out at you. In many cases, something or several things will jump out at you. Just keep in mind that the longer your list is, the better your chances are at finding out what your gift, ability, or skill is. What the heck! You may even find out that you have several gifts, abilities, or skills. Who said that there is a limit to what your gifts, abilities, or skills can be?

Know that if you skimp on making your gift, ability, or skill list, you are only cheating yourself and having a chance at living a happy and prosperous life. What you put into your list is what you will get out of your list. Always remember, "Something from nothing leaves nothing." There are only two guarantees that I know of; **1.** If you are born, you will one day die. **2.** If you never try, you will never succeed at anything in your life. Anything else is a judgment call.

Now that you have your completed list in front of you, it will be up to you to sort through your list and pick out the things or items that you would like to pursue first. I would like to mention that it would not be wise to try to pursue everything on your list at the same time; if you were to do this, you would find yourself overwhelmed and unable to accomplish any of them.

You must learn to focus on one thing at a time until you learn how this process works. No one was born with the knowledge I am sharing with you. So don't act like you were. The only difference between you and successful people would be you. You are the one holding you back.

Successful people do three things that 95% of you have never done or will never do!

Successful people follow their dreams. Successful people are imaginative, creative, inventive, original, ingenious, inspired, artistic, and resourceful individuals. They never allow anyone to talk their dreams down.

Successful people set goals to accomplish their dreams-Successful people write down their thoughts and create a game plan to achieve their desired outcome. You must learn to become goal oriented. You must stop being lazy and overcome procrastination in your life. If you fail to do this, you will never accomplish anything worth accomplishing in your life. If you don't know how to do something, then ask someone who knows. How simple can that be? This is not rocket science! So, stop trying to justify and rationalize it. There is no need to challenge or obfuscate this simple proven statistic. It is what it is and nothing more.

Successful people understand the true meaning of pursuing their dreams- Successful people believe in perseverance, determination, heroism, insistence, resolution, purpose, and diligence. Successful people pursue their dream with an immeasurable passion until they see their vision or dream completed. There is no fiddle-farting around when it comes to what they want to accomplish. Successful people only see the end result and see failure as, not an option they are willing to accept or entertain.

These three things are the keys to being successful in your life. As you can see, there is nothing difficult to this simple equation. The only thing that makes this equation insoluble would be you making it insoluble. Here are the action steps that must be taken for success!

- **You must take action.**
- **Seek knowledge.**
- **Internalize it.**
- **Commit to it.**
- **Implement it.**
- **Apply it.**

I truly believe that 95% of you don't purposely plan to fail but fail to plan your escape route from yourself. When it is all said and done, it will all come down to you and no one else. <u>**No matter what happens in your life, may it be good or bad, will be a direct result of something you did, did not do, should've done or shouldn't have done. You must learn to take credit as well as the blame when it comes to your life**</u>. Any other reasoning is unacceptable!

CHAPTER TWO
OBTAINING QUALIFIED ADVICE

If you continue to do what you've always done
You will continue to be what you've always been.
-Dr. Mark L. Huddleston PhD

I am very passionate about what I am about to cover in this chapter. I feel that too many people in this world follow unqualified individuals. I have always wondered about this phenomenon and how this came to be. I have experienced and witnessed countless times how so many of us can be derailed by fools and imbeciles. Instead of following people that are successful, we are so inclined to conform and be nothing.

I would rather follow a person that has done it already than take the hand of a fool that has no clue, but time and time again, I see person after person conform and listen to unknowledgeable people that have been nowhere and accomplished nothing whatsoever in their lifetime.

It is as if these losers are magnets. People seem to be drawn to them. I truly feel the reason why so many people choose to follow these types of people is due to them being afraid to fight for what they want in life. ***It is much easier to give up without trying than to take a stand and fight for what you want in life.*** *…Dr. Mark Huddleston*

95% of all the people in the world conform to these types of people. You have heard the aphorism before, "Monkey see, Monkey do." Well, that is what 95% of the people in the world do day after day. People follow the follower and don't even know why they do it. Yet, when asked why they conform, most people say, "I have no idea." "I just do it because everyone else does it." That's scary! And you wonder why the world is in the shape it's in.

I want to share a story with you about a real-life scenario that took place within one of my business ventures. I was building a financial services business and was recruiting prospects in the general area. I have always been a good judge of people in general. I always asked the same three questions when interviewing a possible prospect that showed interest in the business opportunity. Those three questions went something like this:

- Do you feel you are **<u>coachable</u>**?
- Do you feel you are **<u>trainable</u>**?
- Do you feel you are **<u>stickable</u>**?

All interested prospects said the same thing time after time that they were **coachable, trainable,** and **stickable.** For those of you that are wondering what stickable means, it means "will you" stick around long enough to be coached and trained. And time after time, the prospect would state that they were all three.

To my amazement, repeatedly, one after another would begin to listen to one of the losers of the group. You know the people I'm writing about. The people that want to do it their way, the people that have all the answers but zero results, and the people that feel the system failed them without even trying to follow a proven system in place.

These types of people have a long track record of failure. They wander around aimlessly from job to job, placing the blame for their failures on their co-workers, supervisors, managers, and the products and services. If it's not one thing, it's another, but the outcome is the same. They know it all but never make the grade.

Somehow these pathetic, pitiful losers gain a following. They seem to be able to brainwash and manipulate people around them to follow their miserable existence. The reason why I told you about this story was to prove a point. What qualifies a person to give you information, may it be good or bad? Why should you listen to a person that is not living the life that you want to live? Is that person successful? Is that person knowledgeable of the information that you seek? Is that person an optimist or a pessimist? These are some of the questions you must ask yourself before allowing someone to mentor you or derail your goals and dreams. It is too easy to obtain the wrong information nowadays.

It is my opinion that you should always go to the source to find the answer to your questions. I never take the word of someone else that is not a specialist in the field of the information I seek. I never conform. I learned long ago that if you go the opposite way of the majority, you are better off in the long run. If the majority of the people in the world are wrong, then the minority of the people would have to be right.

If a person tells you not to do something when you think it would be in your best interest, you should evaluate that request questionably. In most cases, you would be right, and that person's request would be wrong. Never forget that misery loves company. Know that everyone in the world does not wish you well. And most of all, no one wants to be left behind. So, if you feel that it would be in your best interest to do something and someone tells you not to do it, do it anyway. If a person can't justify his request, you should discontinue corresponding with that individual altogether.

I have witnessed thousands upon thousands of people lose out on their goals and dreams due to following the advice of unqualified people. For example: why would you go to a gardener to have your house built? This would be disastrous. You should go to an architect to have them draw up the blueprints for the house you want to build and develop. Then you would choose a general contractor to do the actual building of the home. So why wouldn't you do this in regard to anything else in your life? They say that you would be considered insane if you continued to do the same thing over and over again, expecting a different result each time you do it, so why do it?

You must protect what your mind absorbs, may it be from what you read, what you watch, to what you are being told by others. Garbage in, garbage stays! You must also be careful of what you find on the internet. I have been told many times that the internet is the bathroom wall of the 21st century. Everything you find on the internet is not truthful. Once again, what qualifies the information that you find on the internet? The internet is saturated with pitiful, pathetic losers. I read statements that are made by these ignorant losers time and time again, and I wonder how they even wake up in the morning. Half of them can't read or write, let alone comprehend the subject matter they are commenting on. From their comments, you can tell that they don't have a clue about anything in life at all. "**It is best**

for one to keep their mouth shut and have everyone wonder how intelligent they are than to open their mouth and erase all doubt." Idiots should take these words to heart.

Part of the problem is that most people get advice from people that are struggling and have given up on life. Most of the advice we get about anything is from people close to us who either don't have the information we seek or only have minimal knowledge of the information we seek.

You must look beyond the nonsensical advice of so-called TV experts, family members, blogs, and get-rich articles on Twitter, Facebook, and Instagram. You must look beyond the hype and false propaganda that is out there and select a group of people who have a track record of being successful and knowledgeable in the areas you seek answers to.

Only these people should you seek advice from or model yourself after. You must be very selective about where you get your information from. Never take advice from a pessimist or a false perpetrator. There are many false perpetrators out there; you must avoid them at all costs.

The reason why I am sharing all of this with you is that when I was younger, I had amassed two small fortunes. I relied on advice from people that were not doing as well as I was doing. They say you are a product of your surroundings. That is somewhat true to a point. I originally learned from my immediate surroundings and environment. I adopted the mindset and philosophies of those I looked up to.

The fact of the matter was that the people I looked up to had no business sense whatsoever. They worked hard, and in many cases, they worked two jobs to make ends meet. My father worked two jobs and would squander away any money he had left over after paying bills on drinking. My mother, on the other hand, did not drink, but she would squander her money away on gambling. I often wondered what was the worst of the two evils.

I mentioned in previous books about the story of "**Only Those People**." This story has captured the attention of many of my followers, for they all could relate to this story. I found out that I was not the only person to hear such utter nonsense.

I mentioned earlier that I had amassed two small fortunes in my early life. The reason why I squandered away those fortunes was due to me listening to unknowledgeable people. One of those people was my father. I had asked my father how to invest my fortune, and he showed me how to spend it all. Let the truth be known that my father had no sense of business whatsoever. Why did I ask for advice from him regarding investing? Maybe because I looked up to him. The moral of this story is that I should have sought advice from a qualified, proven professional. I learned to go straight to the source when seeking information.

The raw reality would be that most of us have been raised on incorrect knowledge of almost everything we now know. We are a product of our parent's or guardians' thinking. If you are brought up poor or middle class, you inherit the mindset of those social classes. You cannot outlive what you don't know. Life is not as complicated as parents, guardians, or schools make it out to be. We make things complicated by our own thinking and ignorance.

I am sure all of you know people that have not amounted to much of anything in their life. They tell you things like money can't make you happy. There is no such thing as a good marriage. Let me be the first to tell you that if anyone has ever told you such things, has never experienced such things. These ideas are inherited from those who try to rationalize and make sense of what they don't have. These types of people try to make sense of their situations in life.

I worked with two unscrupulous scoundrels in Northern California. Both their lives and marriages were falling apart due to them lacking ethics, morals, values, and integrity. They were always looking for people to justify their thinking and behavior.

You see, these two unscrupulous scoundrels were stuck with the belief that something positive could come from something negative. They still, to this day, think that doing wrong is doing good. This is what most people do – they try to defend what they have done to survive and then get stuck in a worse situation. Now keep in mind that they caused all these problems themselves. This was all their own doing with no help from anyone else.

These two individuals unquestionably obtained their information on how to conduct themselves in society from unscrupulous scoundrels like themselves. Where you obtain your information knows no bounds. Knowledge does not discriminate against age or sex and doesn't care about your life history. It shows no sympathy and has no feelings. It listens to no one. There is no age too young or too old: Truth! Anyone can obtain knowledge; the secret is to obtain the right knowledge from the right people.

CHAPTER THREE
CONQUERING FEAR

If there was ever a time in this country when men and
women needed to recognize the power of their own
minds and how they could overcome frustration and
fear, that time is now. There is too much fear spread
around, and too many people talking about depression.
Let's get our minds fixed upon a definite goal so big and
so outstanding that we'll have no time to think about
the things we don't want but the things we do want.

-Napoleon Hill

There is no emotion more pernicious than fear. It can make
us feel like the ground has been pulled out from underneath us, and we are spiraling out of control. It can cause us to
question our understanding of ourselves and the world. It roots
itself deep in the subconscious and darkens our dominating
thoughts, coloring our perceptions and, in turn, our actions.
However, fear is a feeling that can be mastered and channeled
to work for us rather than against us.

Have you ever stood face to face with the person, place, or thing that you feared most? Have you ever challenged yourself to overcome your greatest fears, doubts, and insecurities? How often have you confronted the biggest obstacles in your life?

Chances are, you are afraid. Granted, it doesn't happen all the time, and it doesn't happen wherever you go. But it does happen. May the truth be told, this is hindering you from accomplishing your dreams, goals, and ambitions.

You must stop with those lame excuses. You must bust out of those self-made prisons you have created to avoid those things that challenge you or make you uncomfortable. You must stop selling yourself short. You must stop telling yourself that being mediocre is acceptable due to your inability to conquer the fear that other people have conquered.

It is time to stop living in fear!
It is time for transformation!

Know that success is what you make it. You don't have to be a millionaire to be considered successful, just as you don't have to spend every day living paycheck to paycheck to be unsuccessful. True success stems from an ability to know two things: Firstly, that you have satisfied your basic needs, and secondly, that you have provided yourself and those you care about with the tools and means to be successful.

This means the authorization to pursue passions, exercise creativity, and navigate ethics, morals, and values while doing so with integrity. Without self-authorization and personal freedom, true success can never be attained.

Another reason for the lack of success is due to a lack of self-awareness. People often fail to become successful because they fail to find out who they are and what they are capable of. They lack emotional intelligence. They never quite comprehend what inspires, motivates, and keeps them vivacious and happy, along with feeling valuable and significant.

The average person will often slither through life, accepting things as good enough, even when such things are far from what's desired.

I'm sure you want to know what happens.

It's pretty simple. If a person continues along the path of mediocrity, existing but not living, life begins to lose its value. Everyday events become ho-hum and dull. You may tell yourself that you are content and comfortable, but the truth of the matter is more haunting than first thought. Many times, the only reason people feel comfortable is due to them never being uncomfortable.

They settle. They have accepted one way of life. That way of life is mediocrity. For most people, settling is the status quo. People hide in self-made prisons and rarely bother to expand. Settling is a result of fears, doubts, and insecurities that lead us to give up on being as happy as we could or should be. When people settle, they lose track of what matters. Even worse, those people forget what excites them anymore.

Moments of triumph go unnoticed, and the hours, days, weeks, months, and years of life meld together. Ultimately, a deep, heavy, unending fog replaces the potential for happiness and security. In the end, these people get up, go to work, get home, shower, rinse, go to sleep, and repeat. And the miserable cycle continues.

It does not have to be this way. What if you can conquer all your fears and use your fears to catapult yourself to a higher plane? To claim success and personal freedom once and for all. To develop a life without regret. I know this sounds good, but it is actually possible. You can turn those debilitating fears into allies.

Still doubtful? That's ok! I don't expect to change your present philosophy overnight. Just hear me out and give yourself a chance to learn something extraordinary and new.

I know that deep down inside, you would like to own a home to call your own. Later on, in this book, I will cover why owning your own home is better than renting a home from someone else. But right now, I will explain why most people fail when it comes to owning their own home.

I know that many of you have failed at doing something before. I know it is not a great feeling to fail at something. Did you know that there is no such thing as failure unless you give up and stop trying? I have taken the "word" failure out of my vocabulary. I compare failure to "Life Lessons." I truly believe that everyone on this planet learns lessons on a continuous basis.

Let me be bluntly honest with you. Too many people have a **fear** of failing. This is the true reason why most people can't get things going in their lives. Even worse, too many people fear admitting they fear things. So, what do they do? Easy, they lie. They put up a wall. They hide the truth, stretch the facts, and avoid coming to grips with their own demons.

Instead of going after what they really want, they suppress it. They tell themselves that something isn't worth doing because they're not good at it. They tell themselves. That a task is too long, too hard, or too far outside their grasp. They fill themselves with negative affirmations so that they don't feel so bad so that they have a reason for being less than they could be.

The truth of the matter is that it's a common practice and one that gets us nowhere in life. The reason so many people give up prematurely or don't even try at all is because of that little thing called fear. People fear failing at something. When we think of failure, we think of frailty. We imagine not paying our bills on time, never reaching our dreams, and never getting the girl or guy, woman or man, wife or husband, house or car that we desire.

By and large, the fear of failure represents finality. It represents an end to what was once a gleaming possibility, It represents an inability to get what we want. And in the end, the thought of inability haunts us.

But why? Why do so many people crawl through life afraid of monsters and ghosts? What is it that causes a person to break down and give up because of so-called failure? The answer is FEAR! The average person does not see the truth. In truth, failure is neither good nor bad. Failures are merely lessons to be learned to get to where we are going in life. Whether breaking up with that special someone, losing your wallet while shopping, or some other life trial or tribulation, failure is as normal and abundant as air.

Think of all the times you have struggled and didn't succeed immediately or didn't get something right on the first try. Do you consider these scenarios failures? Do you consider small things like learning how to walk and falling down or learning how to ride a bike and falling over failing? Do you consider getting 70% on a test failing?

The reason for these questions should be quite obvious. How you deal with failure depends on the perception of who you are and how you were raised. Failure can mean anything. It can range from the slightest conceivable mistake to the largest blunder, such as gambling your life savings away or falling asleep while smoking in bed and burning down the complex you live in or losing your livelihood due to some transgression.

Failure can be anything due to no person being perfect. This means that we have all failed many times before and will continue to fail at other things. This means there is only one thing you can do. Erase failure from your fear list. Forget the idea of failure altogether. It is a pessimistic term. It is negative, counterproductive, and frankly overused. Messing up every now and then is not going to change. There is no reason to give up on life and beat yourself up repeatedly.

If you consider yourself incapable, you are creating what is called a self-fulfilling prophecy. It means that you expect it, so you make it happen. By thinking of yourself as a failure, you begin to try less. Your mood is diminished, your zest for life is depleted, and you generally go about things with less attention to detail. You feel like, Why try? You'll still be a failure, right?

Wrong! The only time you'll be a failure is if you don't try and give up. Failures are not people who fight and get knocked down and get up again. Failures are people who get knocked down and stay down. Failures are people that always whine, bitch, and moan about how unfair things are without ever making an effort to change them.

Failures are people who give up. They worship mediocrity while shoveling convenient excuses down your throat and the throat of any poor sap who will listen. The reason that certain people become failures is that they take the road most traveled.

Instead of addressing their fears, they worry about losing face. You see these types of people everywhere you go. Weak men and women. Fearful messes who can't control a thing in their life and blame outside circumstances for everything that happens in their life.

Many are poor, drunk, or drugged-out losers who choose to numb themselves because they don't have the heart and courage to change. These average washouts who once had dreams and aspirations now refer back to their past successes, supposedly content with living a mediocre life full of regrets.

Please don't think that I am insensitive; because I'm not. Failures are people who stop trying. All others, however, are not failures. There are many people who mess up despite trying and adapting to their errors and mistakes. Just know that those errors and mistakes are not failures; they are lessons. And everyone goes through them.

Every time you can't do something the way you want it done, you have learned a lesson. Whether it is as simple as learning that a task is difficult or as tricky or as deep as gaining some profound insight, every lesson is noteworthy.

Know that there is a process to getting what you want and that few things happen overnight. And when they are, they often go unappreciated. This is why children born into money are predisposed to chronic boredom, behavioral issues, and substance abuse. This is why men and women don't respect one another when sex comes easy. This is also why people used to always getting what they want, struggle with impulse control, and not enjoying parts of life that are not instantly gratifying.

Take what I am about to share with you to heart. When people get what they want immediately, they don't value it. They have no concept of what it takes to get it or earn it. They struggle to see the point of something if that something is merely handed to them. It has no meaning and no relation to their efforts and abilities; therefore, they expect it and abuse it.

Once again, this is why life imparts lessons. You won't learn how important it is to be on time for your job until you've been reprimanded or fired. You won't learn what it takes to get the career of your dreams until you have struggled, been turned down, doubted, chewed out, and underutilized. How would you be able to appreciate anything good if you have not gone through anything bad?

You can't know what it takes to do anything without having gone through the steps. Step by step, lesson by lesson. You are not failing when you don't immediately get what you want. You're learning. And with each progressive hurdle cleared, you're succeeding. You're moving further along that trajectory toward your goals and accomplishments. Without obstacles, we would never have the motivation to do anything.

Difficulty hardens us and gives us wisdom. Without difficulty, we weaken. Only the weak would choose not to strive for more. Only those who give up on their dreams are failures. Anyone else, no matter how tireless or unsuccessful in their efforts are, learning.

I know for a fact that success, not failure, can scare us the most. I have mentioned that many people fear failure. It's embarrassing, it's devastating, and it leaves us doubting ourselves. I get it. We all know of fearing failure, but how many of us bring up the opposite of failure? I have seen people fear success on many occasions.

Success is a powerful force that can bring out the best or the worst in someone. Success can be the gateway to feeling great about yourself and waking up every day with a sense of purpose and promise. If it were not for success or the idea of being successful, no one would have anything to strive for.

Never lose sight that success does not have to mean monetary success. Having the financial stability to do what you want is only a small part of the equation. And that's the point I am trying to make. People like doing what they want. Some people can never have enough of anything and never be happy. Others can live on a farm in the middle of nowhere and be happier than a speckled pup pulling a red wagon on the 4th of July.

When we are successful, we have found a life or lifestyle that is not only suitable but rewarding. We have discovered a place where an openness to life replaces fear and insecurity.

Unfortunately, most of us don't reach the success we desire. One of the main reasons why we don't achieve the success we desire would be due to us being afraid of making it happen. Think about it for a second. Success is scary. When you are successful, you are exposed for everyone to see. More than that, success is biochemically similar to fear. When we are afraid of something, our minds trigger the fight or flight mechanism in which we either flee for dear life or take the challenge head-on.

When the chain of fear is activated, your mind can perceive that something very simple can literally be a life-or-death issue. With that said, fear can also seem very much like the feelings we get with newfound success. When we first experience a sense of new success, our body chemistry changes. As in fear, our breathing picks up, our heart rate increases, we perspire more, and our instincts take over. In either situation, whether outright terrified or nervous about being successful, all of us will always experience an initial rush or euphoria.

Many people cannot handle the exhilaration. The number one reason for fear of success is the fear of the unknown. As I mentioned earlier, success may mean that you're finally out there in the open, more exposed, more powerful, but also very vulnerable. There may be more demands and pressures. If you get promoted to a higher position, the pay may be higher, but so too are the expectations. Many people fear that their lack of skills will be exposed, and they will not be able to live up to the expectations of the employer or that they will end up ensnared in a new life that they were unprepared for.

Granted, we are creatures of habit, so when something good happens, we don't know how to react. Yes, we can be happy, but we can also be uncertain. When we get used to something, even if that something is not objectively good or even pleasant, we become reluctant to change. We find familiarity in the old ways of doing things and experiencing things, and so new ways seem threatening.

Embracing success can be remedied. You need only remind yourself of the things you are gaining, the things you always wanted and are now doubting. Make a list of mental notes on a pad of paper, cell phone, or computer as a reminder. Remind yourself of the benefits of accomplishing whatever you want to accomplish. Think of self-esteem, monetary gain, prestige, and a sense of accomplishment. Think of the end result. Think of lying on your bed or couch in your new home. Feeling wonderful about what you have accomplished.

You must find a **motive** that will keep you energized and focused. And if you make it, that will make all the difference in the world. Getting that new home will be just a small fragment of what really matters. Overcoming your fear of success will outweigh any negative scenario you may encounter. Overcoming your fear of success means understanding the consequences of that success.

Others may put you down and judge you. While others may try their best to misguide you. Don't forget about the haters and so-called know-it-alls who will tell you how to live your life. Trust me when I tell you that misery loves company. Most of your so-called friends who are not going anywhere in life will try their best to talk you out of accomplishing your goals. May it be buying a home or anything else that will benefit you. Do you want to know why? It will be because they will be left behind with no one to share their grief, pain, and misery. They will have one less person to attend their self-pity parties.

Don't let people make you feel guilty about making your dreams come true. People will tell you that you forgot where you came from or that you think you are better than us now. The fact of the matter is that you have not forgotten who you are. The only thing that will change will be your desire to live the good life instead of whining and crying about not having anyone or anything. Let us not forget that you will be better than them in the end. You will have your own home and whatever else you wish to have.

I've seen it all before. You get what you've always wanted, then all the previous doubters come out of the woodwork and lay on the heavy guilt trip of how terrible you have become, how you have forgotten your old friends, and how you think you are better than everyone else.

Don't think of becoming successful as losing your old self but as gaining a new and improved self. You shooting for the moon is an opportunity to explore new avenues for growth. It also gives you a chance to cultivate new skills, try on new hats, and pursue new passions.

One fear that many people don't like to talk about would be the fear of being controlled. I know you have heard of people fearing the unknown, but fearing being controlled is another monster. Many people love to live in their comfort zone. When life begins to get away from you, life can become random, incomprehensible, and unexpected.

However, that doesn't mean that there can't be meaning to all the madness. For instance, the belief of a devout religious person believes that life is channeled through various ways. They believe that a higher power is at the controls, deciding what happens and when things happen. Many religious people believe that you must have faith in where the higher power directs you. With faith, everything has some significance, some meaning, which means that life's unknowns are not to be feared but to be trusted. They also believe that everything happens for a reason.

As I mentioned earlier, it is not the unknown that many of us fear but the uncontrolled. Just think about it for a second. There are plenty of things that we don't know that we don't think about, let alone fear. We fear those things that we know about that we are able to comprehend, even if we aren't sure of the details. The reason that we fear these things is because they make us feel panicked and uncertain.

Have you ever felt like so much of your life was seemingly out of control? As if the vast majority of everyday people, places, and things continued to elude your grasp. What if something happened to you or your friends or loved ones? What if there was some health mishap, lost relationship, death or injury, or monetary downfall? What if you suddenly lost the capability to do what you had always loved or dreamed of doing?

All the scenarios mentioned would scare us. Not the unknown but the uncontrolled. When something is outside of our control, we feel helpless. Many become so incapacitated by their fears that they abuse drugs, numbing and destroying themselves in order to escape the reality of uncertainty. Other people approach life more objectively. They assess the risks, they plan for the future, they try to rely on pragmatic evidence and hard research to determine the best course of action in any given situation. Others try not to control much, and they let things come as they do. They reduce their stress by hoping for the best while acknowledging that bad things can and do occur.

Ultimately, it all depends on the person's life up to this point. The outlook hinges upon the individual's environment and background, as well as his or her current philosophy. The important thing to remember is that not everything can be controlled. Fearing the uncontrolled means wasting time that could be spent doing other things. In order to overcome your fear of the uncontrolled and in order to avoid becoming an obsessed control freak, it is best to be realistic.

You must hold yourself accountable and responsible. Never lose sight that each goal should indicate something that you consider under your control. If your goal seems too stringent at first, create sub-goals, then break those sub-goals down into manageable tasks. For example, if you want to buy a house, you should first go down to several banks or loan originators and inquire about what requirements will be needed to apply for a home loan with them. That would be the first place to start. When doing so, you will want to sit down with a licensed loan officer, **not a financial representative**.

You may get rejected for a home loan or something else that you desire very much. Just know that, in many cases, that rejection can lead to reason. Here is a metaphor that may help you understand this point more clearly. If life always offered you lemons, you would be sitting around all day making lemonade. How can you get the house that you want if you are all caught up in making lemonade?

The point I'm trying to convey is that sometimes life is better with a little adversity. When you are rejected by a partner, rejected by a school, by a job or field, by certain banks, or denied by certain clubs or groups, no matter the form of rejection, getting turned down can be a very good motivator.

Conversely, rejection is one of the main developmental stepping-stones for men and women, especially future dominant males and females. The truth is when we are rejected, we learn several things. The first thing we learn is that we learn that life is not perfect, and neither are we. The second thing we learn is that things don't always go our way. The third thing we learn is that opinions differ, and behaviors vary. The fourth thing we learn is that rejection is potentially advantageous.

Think about it: not all things in life will line up, and all opportunities can't be taken advantage of. Sometimes, people, places, and things are not compatible, and it's nobody's fault. Sometimes, the way of the world allows us to see that one missed opportunity creates another. Think about it another way; if you don't get what you want, maybe it's a blessing in disguise. Take, for instance, a man who gets turned down for a job. Instead of getting the job, he gets depressed about his prospects, heads to the liquor store, and picks up a bottle of gin while he is at the liquor store, he meets his future wife. That may sound a little far-fetched, but things like this have been known to happen. What's important to remember is that you never know what life will throw your way. Even if you don't believe in a higher power or a grander plan, you can still view rejections in a positive light. If you change your approach or style due to one or more rejections, you may just end up pursuing things you never knew you were good at, experiences you never knew you would enjoy, or going places you never imagined you would end up.

Rejection is a process of growth that is very important. From rejection comes reason. Although many of us may act emotionally at first, the best approach is to think rationally. Know that rejection cannot hurt you. It matters how you look at the rejection. I know you are wondering how rejection can strengthen you and your determination. Just know it can.

There is another facet of fear I would like to share with you. It would be the understanding of who we are. Let's start by realizing that life is wonderful and great and that it is this mind shift and this understanding that brings us to an important truth.

Fear is all about loss. Consider everything you have ever feared, whether it be monsters in your closet as a kid or your dwindling savings account, or whatever makes you worry or stay up at night. It's probably got something to do with loss. We fear losing ourselves. We fear losing our sight, we fear losing our health, and our ability to do all the things we want to do.

We fear losing the ability to care for ourselves and the people that we love and care for.

We fear losing our position in life. Maybe you have a nice career, or you are in good social standing, or maybe you have made cool and exciting friendships. Whatever the case, it has probably crossed your mind from time to time what it would be like not to have any of those things. If anybody's ever told you not to "take for granted" what you have, then you know there's a lot of loss to fear.

Money is another big one. We fear losing a reliable stream of income, being unable to pay our bills, and afford nice things and conveniences like cable TV, portable tablets, other appliances, and cars. We fear losing our retirement, not saving wisely, investing in the wrong asset classes and market sectors, being swindled, and being lured into a business opportunity that turns out to be a scam.

Many people simply fear losing a sense of inner peace. For those who do not practice mindfulness, a sense of peace may be hard to come by. We don't know what to think at times because our mind is moving all the time and never slows down. Others find it difficult to keep their mind in check by resisting the comforting call of daydreams, and many more are diagnosed with ADHD.

Peace of mind is often tied directly to our sense of loss. If we feel that we've lost too much or have too much to lose, we may seize up. This emotional paralysis can manifest as detachment from everyday life, as depression, and even as irritability or hostility. Some people will try to disguise this problem through substance abuse, but more often than not, there is nothing they can do.

Another sense of loss is that of looks. The cosmetic and plastic surgery industries have made billions in this area. They know that people are naturally insecure about their looks. The main reason is that people want to be received well by others. People also want to receive themselves well. They don't want to look in the mirror and be reminded of the years of stress that have worn on them. They don't want to be reminded that they are going to eventually die.

Basically, everybody fears potential loss, and it is this potential loss that creates issues with everyday living. What people must realize is that there is always a potential for loss. In any situation, under any circumstance, something can go wrong. Preparing for such a loss is reasonable and expected, but the probability of loss will never cease to exist.

<u>Loss is based upon possession. You can't lose what you don't personally possess.</u> This is why many people get stuck. They feel that if they progress too far, they might become too vulnerable.

They will suddenly have something worth having, and losing that something, whether it be a person, place, or thing, can be devastating.

But devastation is not the only outcome. Losing something can lead to gaining something greater. The mere experience of possessing something can be so rewarding that even when that possession ends, the memories will endure. Again, it all comes back to accepting life as a process, and this can be difficult for people who are crippled emotionally and mentally, or even physically.

When something is lost, sometimes it is for the best. We all grow. We all get older and amass more experiences and learn more about ourselves and the world. Fearing what we want and need is not right and should never be tolerated. <u>You do not experience life when you fear living!</u>

You must go after what you want and don't think of it as failing or falling flat on your face. If you don't get it right away, that's ok. And once you get it, don't fear losing it. Do you know what's even scarier than losing something invaluable or losing somebody invaluable? It would be a person who has never had anybody or anything because what kind of person would ever want that?

The next type of fear would be something that we all suffer from every now and then. This type of fear would be the lies we tell ourselves. This is one of the most destructive fears. You need to accept one fact. No one cares more about what happens to you than you. You may deny it, or you may put on a front like nothing matters to you. You may act selfless, but at the end of the day, the only person who lives your life is you.

No one loves you more than you love yourself. The only person who loves your life is you! People may feel for you or love you, but they don't experience life as you do. This is because they aren't you. So, it is up to you to understand who you are. You have the biggest effect on yourself. When you accomplish things in your life, you are doing them because you want to and because you need to. You pay your bills because you must. You go to the doctor because you have to or want to. You become part of certain social groups, shop at certain stores, go to certain restaurants, drive on certain roads, and take on certain hobbies because you have decided to do so, whether it is something you want to do or need to do.

It's ok to be self-centered. We all are at times. This doesn't mean that you ignore other people; it just means that you generally strive to do what's best for you. In many cases, that's also what is best for others. This is why you and you alone can be your worst enemy or your best friend.

Do you ever struggle with self-love? Do you ever find self-love to be a difficult or impossible task? Do you want to accept your imperfections and stop getting in your own way? If you do, you must realize that the power is in you to do so. Not your family, not your friends, not some expert on TV, not even me.

All of the people mentioned may help, but ultimately the decision is up to you. This is why you must treat yourself right. And it all begins with honesty. You must be honest with yourself. If you are not achieving what you want, you must admit it and move on. Don't sit around sulking and wallowing in self-pity. Don't ask for help from unqualified individuals or individuals who are unwilling to give you the information you seek, and certainly don't try to avoid your problems through substance abuse or self-destructive behaviors.

Whatever you do, don't lie to yourself. This is the trap that most people get caught in. When lying to somebody else, their perspective of you may change. If they don't know that you are lying, you are going to feel bad at some point, especially if they mean something to you. Even if they don't mean anything to you, you may still feel bad. You may find that you are losing your ethics, morals, values, or sense of self.

Most people who buy a home will lose it quickly due to lying to themselves. There is nothing worse than lying to ourselves. When we lie to ourselves, we try to convince ourselves of something we know not to be true. We try to force ourselves into unreal situations or circumstances. We try to be something that seems somehow contrary to our nature, to what we want and need from our lives.

When we lie to ourselves, we are also lying to everybody else outside us because we are deceiving them by being what we are not. There is nothing scarier than a person who is too insecure ever to reveal their true self. And at the end of the day, this is what fear is all about. We fear not being able to be our true selves, to live life with the vision we have in mind, with the people we want and need, and with the lifestyle and trajectory that makes us secure.

In order to first conquer our fears or any fears, we must first conquer ourselves. You must understand that fear stems from the external world and its numerous problems and pitfalls from your inner world. It is your inner world that allows you to interact with the external world. Your thoughts and feelings, attitudes and mindsets, behaviors, and output all modulate the external world within the realm of human possibility.

If you can navigate your daily life, aligning both external and internal worlds, then you can navigate even the choppiest of waters. You know what you have to do. Make a difference in your life today by becoming the person you want to be tomorrow. I know you can do it! I know that you can make progress. And with time and grace, you may just find that your greatest insecurities are also your greatest strengths.

I know I spent a lot of time focusing on this chapter. Fear can prevent you from living your dreams. It can prevent you from doing the necessary footwork to make buying your first home successful. Face your fear and always be true to yourself and your situations.

CHAPTER FOUR
BUYING VS. RENTING

I would rather shoot for the moon and miss,
then aim for the gutter and make it!
-My Grand-Mother

Buying a home may be the biggest financial decision many people will make. As with any major decision, a key question to answer before continuing would be: **Why**?

Perhaps your **Why** is a larger home to raise children, or have a yard, or get to a better school system, or in the time of COVID-19, to find a home office. There is no right or wrong answer, merely the best one that fits each individual circumstance.

There is an emotional side to home ownership, particularly in the United States – we have been mentally conditioned that owning your own home is the American dream, and it does feel good to own your own home instead of just occupying a temporary dwelling."

Not a day goes by without me hearing the question, "Is buying a home better than renting?" The simple answer would be yes! As I mentioned earlier, like anything else in life, it depends on your specific situation. Some of the factors you should consider would be how long you plan on living at the home you want to buy, your debt-to-income ratio, and market conditions, just to name a few.

The benefits of homeownership don't come without costs and limitations. For some, renting may be a better option. The pros and cons of buying a house should be considered as you think through the process and before a decision is made.

Overall, buying a home sets you on the path to financial freedom. So, yes, if you are able to make it happen, **buying is a better choice than renting**. Here's why!

The COVID-19 pandemic lit the housing market like a bottle rocket. Home prices rose in early 2021 at the fastest pace in 15 years. The most affordable homes rose 16.5% year over year. Homes are being bought up at lightning speed due to this buyers' market.

The boom in sales and buying is expected to continue for several more years at most. It's great for sellers, provided they have found a home they can afford to buy. It's not so great for those who may not be able to afford a down payment or who can't act fast enough. Buyers well-positioned to make an offer can find their dream home; they just have to act quickly. In this housing market, there is no reward in hesitating.

Let's talk about **property appreciation**. There is only so much land available. The boundedness of land resources is one reason real estate investors always emphasize "location, location, location." There are only so many homes you can fit in Marin County. FYI, Marin County is one of the richest counties in America. It is also located in California, right outside of San Francisco. Most of the land in Marin County is bought up.

The simple economic law of supply and demand keeps property prices and rent rising so long as the demand remains high.

The extremely limited space within Marin County drives the property value up faster and faster. Don't forget about the weather. There is no snow in Marin County, nor are there tornados, hurricanes, or major flooding.

California is the place to be. The real estate market continues to rise due to the demand to live there. The cost of living is 41% higher than the national average. Housing is 96% higher than the national average. Since the 1940s, the United States population has doubled, and the median home price has quadrupled in value. The short-term growth rates may change; however, the long-term trajectory is clear.

Building Equity – As a renter, you can easily spend half a million dollars or more on rent over the years. $1,500 a month for 30 years comes to approximately $540,000, and in the end, you will wind up just where you started—owning nothing. Or you can buy a house and spend the same amount paying down a mortgage, and in the end, wind up owning your own home free and clear.

If you can manage the down payment, you will save yourself and your family from a substantial financial burden in the long term by buying rather than renting. I suggest that you shop around to see if there are first-time buyer programs in your area. There are also down payment assistance programs out there. But you must do the groundwork to utilize one of them. Or you can go at it the traditional way and come up with 20% of the overall purchasing price required as a down payment. You just make payments as if you're paying rent. The major difference is that by buying, you will become a property owner with lucrative tax-deductible benefits. Think hard. Everyone needs a place to live. If you don't own a home, you will have to rent. This is a no-brainer. Why not let your monthly payments work for you?

On a 30-year fixed mortgage, your payment will be a flat rate every month. That payment is split between (PITI) principle, interest, taxes, and insurance. (escrow). Each month, the interest portion of your mortgage decreases while the principal portion of your mortgage increases. A $375,000 home with 20% down and a 5% interest rate would have an interest and principal payment of $1,610 per month. As time progresses, that would be split as follows.

Sample Payment Table:

Month 1	Month 60	Month 120
Interest: $1,250	Interest: $1,150	Interest: $1,020
Principal: $360	Principle: $460	Principle: $590

When paying a mortgage, you're essentially paying off your loan a little faster each month. Consequently, your net worth increases every month.

Tax Benefits – Real Estate is the most effective way to make money while paying the least amount of taxes. Actually, the American tax system is more favorable to individuals whose primary source of income is derived from capital gains, probably as a way to give people an incentive to invest in properties while promoting "the American Dream." Regardless of the reason, you should take advantage of it.

Paying rent yields no real financial advantages and no tax deductions. Paying your mortgage, on the other hand, offers many financial benefits. Such as any interest you pay on your mortgage is deductible from your taxes. Using the same example from above, a $375,000 home with a 20% down payment and a 5% interest rate would equal $14,900 for one year of interest payments. All of that is tax-deductible. If your state has real estate property taxes, these are most likely tax-deductible as well. Let's say you want to complete a few renovations. Are you planning to paint the house, add a fence, or do any other remodeling that would raise the value of your home? You will want to keep those receipts because the cost of renovations can be deducted from your property gains tax when you sell the property.

Wealth and Security – Did you know that 97% of millionaires are homeowners? They live in homes currently valued at an average of $320,000. Many of those millionaires have occupied the same home for more than 20 years. They have enjoyed significant increases in the value of their homes. It's no coincidence that 97% of millionaires are homeowners. Real estate is one of the most expensive and appreciating assets on the market, and most millionaires use it to not only maintain but to increase their net worth.

Generally, the word investment is associated with real estate or the stock market. Both avenues serve as tried-and-true methods for creating and preserving wealth. But this book is about buying your first home. I presently have my financial securities licenses and a book that goes over stocks and mutual funds. Please pick it up after you purchase your first home.

In this book, I will go over scenarios to help you better understand the benefits of buying a home compared to renting. This will help explain why most millionaires own their homes as opposed to renting a home. I will also show you how purchasing a home saves you money and speeds up your access to being financially secure or even becoming a millionaire yourself. To avoid the excuse of "that's not a realistic comparison." I will reference a personal and real scenario later in this chapter.

Control and Freedom – Becoming a homeowner provides a sense of commitment and accomplishment. Being a homeowner also gives you a feeling of control and freedom. You will never have to worry about the landlord coming into your home in the middle of the day for an inspection. You will never have to worry about defaulting on your lease, reporting to your landlord, negotiating your lease renewal, or seeing an unexpected price jump in your rent payments.

The control part of this equation is wonderful. When you own your home, you can put up a fence around your property for added security. You can paint your house whatever color you like as well as any room in your house. You're in complete control, with no one to answer to. All these benefits and conveniences are invaluable, especially for your saneness.

I have worked with many people who were renting due to them listening to negative myths and misconceptions. After educating those people, they are now proud homeowners. This is the first thing I bring up when talking to renters. "***When will it ever be the right time, if not first you take the time to make some time.***"

I have sat down with many homeowners and asked them when the right time was to buy a home. Many of them stated that there is no perfect time. The right time is NOW! So many people told me that while they were waiting for the right time to buy a house, the right time never came about, and they ended up losing out on building equity. In other words, they missed out on paying themselves. "**Be an owner, not a loaner!**"

Conversely, you can lease a property while looking for a home to buy. If you have a spouse and two kids, you may want to lease a three-bedroom condominium. It will allow you and the kids the space needed to live comfortably.

So now you apply to lease the property. The landlord accepts your application, and you sign a one-year lease agreement. Now, you pay $100 for the application fee and $1,500 for moving costs, and you agree to $2,500 in rental payments across a twelve-month term.

You, your spouse, and the kids like your new place to stay. The schools are close by. Your kids have made friends with the neighbor's kids, and everything seems to be going well. After a year goes by, you decide what the heck. Let's lease it for one more year. All that is left to do is contact the landlord, who is always happy to renew leases with present tenants.

When contacting the landlord, he states that the area's home values have gone up. He agrees to renew the lease but tells you that similar properties are now leasing for $2,700 per month, that's an additional $200 per month or $2,400 a year. While that extra $200 per month may not overwhelm you, it is meaningful when you think of it from an opportunity

cost perspective. With $2,400 a year, you can pick up smart home appliances or change the tile in your bathroom, and a whole lot more.

What choice do you have? Do you pack up and leave and go hunting for a new place to stay? And while looking for a new place to stay, you will have to pay for a hotel or motel room at $100+ a night for as long as it may take to find a new place, and let's not count out the moving costs and the storage costs for all of the things you presently own.

What about the kids? They are in the school next to your present location. Are you ready to pay another $100 lease application fee and another $1,500 moving costs? What about the minor inconveniences like updating driver's licenses, updating bank checks, and even calling the cable company? Who wants to go through that all over again?

It's a tough decision to make. I know $2,700 is a lot of money; however, you really are on the hook if you think about it logically. You sign a new lease agreement, and you're committed to another year. Another year passes by. The kids have settled in and have made lots of friends. Your family's foundation in the local community has become more rooted. You are now contributing your spare time to the neighborhood church.

Now, you are completely attached to your home. Meanwhile, the landlord's property appreciates once more in a strong economy, and one property in the neighborhood sells for a record price. That's all the justification the landlord needs to think his property should be rented for $2,900 per month. That's another $200 increase. This increase could prove to be too much for you and your family this time around.

After much thought, you come to grips with reality and agree that this is too much to pay. When the second year comes to an end, you let the landlord know your intentions. It's just too much. A similar condominium three miles away is on the market for $2,600 a month. The new condo would save you $100 a month from your current $2,700 monthly payment, and staying where you are now would now be $300 a month more expensive. So, you decide that the cost and nuisance of moving are now justified.

After applying for the new condominium, you get accepted. On your move-out day, your previous landlord performs a standard move-out inspection. He spots some cracks in the walls. Some stains on the carpets and some missing door stops. Altogether, it costs $900 to get all of these things taken care of after deducting $900 from the $2,500 security deposit, which leaves you with $1,600 from your original deposit of $2,500.

You have learned much from your mistakes and are much wiser this time around. So, you sign a three-year fixed lease, guaranteeing no escalations above $2,600 for three years. Your new home is a little older than your last home, which is why you got such a good price, but the biggest drawback is that one of your kid's school districts changes during the middle of the school year. Even though that happens, you take pride in the fact that your backyard is much larger than the last condo you lived in.

The much larger backyard helps relieve the distress of moving from your last home. To further ease the separation anxiety, you decide to get a cat to help your kids become acclimated to their new schools and new home. The cat's energy resonates throughout the home and invigorates your kid's spirits. Getting the cat helps with the transition, and the kids don't feel so bad anymore.

Now that you have settled into your new home with the large backyard, all you need now is a fence to add to the security and privacy of your home. So, you call the landlord and plead your case. The only problem is that the landlord doesn't see the value of installing a $3,000 fence. You, being the head of the household, take a moment to analyze your predicament. Do you want to spend $3,000 to build a fence while on a three-year lease?

You must keep in mind that you don't own this property. You only rent. You would be enhancing the value of the landlord's property. Now you come to grips with your situation. Two years prior, you could have used the money you had invested in stocks to put a down payment on your own home and owned it straight out. Instead, your family is forced to adapt to a renter's way of life. So much uncertainty, along with many other modifications unsuitable to your preferences.

I hope this mental illustration paints a vivid picture of what life is like when you decide to rent instead of buying a home. You are never in control when you're renting. In the end, you will always be at the mercy of the landlord's will. As long as the landlord is staying within the terms of the lease, they may inspect the property, market the property, sell it from up under you, renovate it, or take other actions that may be a distraction or inconvenience to you and your family.

If you only plan to live in a home for one or two years, don't buy the home. Wait until you are ready to make a long-term commitment. Price appreciation is a long-term goal. The buying-versus-renting debate is specific to an individual's wants, needs, and situation. From a financial standpoint, you are better off, in the long run, purchasing a home than paying rent. Keep in mind that 97% of millionaires own their homes, not because they are rich, but because buying a home helped them become wealthy.

CHAPTER FIVE

GETTING YOUR
FINANCES IN ORDER

*I find it fascinating that most people can come up with
all kinds of excuses why they can't do something and no
excuses of how they can do something....*

- Dr. Mark L. Huddleston Ph.D.

Hopefully, that last chapter hit a nerve within you. If you have read up to this point means you feel that you have what it takes to take the next step in buying your own home. In this chapter, I will be going over the financial aspects of buying your own home. Don't blink, or you may miss something.

You will want to take good notes in this chapter, for if your finances are out of line, you will not be able to buy your dream home. You must find out just how financially prepared you are. ***If you got it together, you don't have to get it together.***

You will want to prepare your finances to make the buying process as seamless as possible. Take a deep breath and relax. You don't have to be a math wizard to make this happen. All you will have to do is follow these simple steps to get where you want to be.

The first step is to know your financial situation. First and foremost, please stay away from unknowledgeable people. You will want to go straight to the source. When you go to unknowledgeable people, they don't take into account your specific wants and personal needs. Those same people don't know your complete financial situation. Your financial situation may be better than other people's financial situation.

The first thing you should understand is what many lenders are looking for. Your monthly mortgage payment should not exceed 28 percent of your gross monthly income. Let's look at this scenario so you can get a better picture of what I am trying to convey to you. Let's say you and your partner have a dual income of $100,000 with no kids and only $2,000 in additional debt payments per month. The question is, can the two of you afford to spend 28% of your monthly income on a mortgage? To be truthful, there is no way of telling what you can afford. You would have to find out your **income-to-debt ratio** first.

You would need to have a complete picture of your financial situation. Just know that everyone's situation is unique. I would suggest that you sit down with a licensed Real Estate loan officer and/or financial advisor so that they can run the numbers for you. <u>A true financial advisor or real estate loan officer is liable if he or she sets you up with a loan you can't afford.</u>

Here are some things to consider so that you can recognize your unique situation:

✓ You must understand the benefits of becoming a homeowner. Once you understand those benefits, you will know for a fact that it will be worth the investment. If you are still reading along, you are way ahead of the game. Most people would have put this book down and given up by now. So that says a lot about you.

✓ If you are going about owning a home on your own or with someone else, you will have to calculate the amount of the largest down payment that you can make. I also want you to keep in mind that there is down payment assistance out there. You must do your homework. If you are not sure of the amount of down payment you will need, you may want to sit down with a licensed real estate loan officer or loan originator. You will want to take good notes when you sit down with either one. You must be true to yourself. There is no one way of doing anything, but there are a lot of wrong ways of doing them. The truth of the matter is that I have made all the mistakes for you, so you don't have to. You will want to take a snapshot of your financial obligations. Find out what your monthly obligations are. How much discretionary income do you spend? You will want to have a good idea of your financial situation to properly assess what you can afford to put down as a down payment. You will want to be realistic. In other words, you want to own your home, not have your home own you. While buying a home can come with some incredible benefits, spreading yourself thin can cause you plenty of unnecessary stress and anxiety.

✓ When you are meeting with a licensed loan officer or loan originator, you will want to ask them to help calculate your debt-to-income ratio. Your debt-to-income ratio is calculated by dividing your monthly debt obligations by your monthly gross income. The ratio is expressed as a percentage, and lenders use it to determine how well you manage your monthly debts. Your debt-to-income ratio shows a lender if you will be able to repay a loan if given one. The lower your debt-to-income ratio, the more willing a lender will be to do business with you. Now, according to some of the larger home lenders in America, lenders prefer to see a debt-to-loan ratio of less than 36%, with no more than 28% of that debt going toward servicing your mortgage. Once you have calculated your debt-to-income ratio, you will want to work on lowering that ratio if you don't meet the 36% ratio previously stated. You can do this by paying off any small debts you still have open. Once again, if you are still unsure how to calculate your debt-to-income ratio, you can always go to a loan originator or a real estate loan officer, and they will be more than happy to run your number for you. Know that the number one revenue drivers for lenders are credit cards and loans, in that order. So, if you do your part, the lenders will do their part.

✓ Now, you will want to make a list of your fixed expenses. If you can't list your outstanding expenses off the top of your head, you will want to collect all your bills and make a list of them. You will want to add to your list the times your bills are due and their balances. You will want to think long and hard about all your monthly expenditures. Don't forget about subscriptions and necessities, like, phone bills, cable, and Wi-Fi. By going through your statements, you'll be able to make a complete list of your fixed costs. You may even surprise yourself by finding some potential opportunities to save as well.

✓ You will want to analyze where your money is going. Some of you may even know what a financial statement is. By having a financial statement drawn up by a financial advisor, you will get a clear picture of where your money is flowing. Is your money coming into your bank account and leaving right back out? If you are not saving at least 10% of your net income, you may have some lifestyle changes to entertain. A quick overview of your finances can reveal ways to cut back. You will want to take an in-depth look at how much, how frequently, and what you are spending your money on. Many times, this course of action will uncover patterns or trends of which you may not have been aware of. You must gain control of your spending. You will want to develop strong budgeting habits that will ensure that you will reach your ultimate goal. (Owning your own home) If you need help coming up with a livable budget. Check out one of these websites: EveryDollar.com or Mint.com.

✓ Here is something I would like to share with you. I know that a down payment is a large amount of money to come up with. But in the long run, it will be well worth it. I also recommend that you put away some extra money for unexpected problems that may arise along the way. You never know what life will throw at you. Having a six-month emergency fund will give you time to figure out any problems that you may come across.

✓ Understanding the costs associated with buying a home. There are supplemental costs to any sizable purchase. Just like when you buy a new car. You look at the sticker price, and you think that price is what you are going to get the car for. But to your surprise, by the time you walk out of the dealership, the cost of that vehicle could be a substantial amount more. You may want leather bucket seats, wire wheels, and tinted windows. Or perhaps, you may want an extended protection plan, along with other accessories. Another example would be cruise lines and five-star hotels. Many times, they will charge mandatory service fees. The same is true when buying a home. Added fees can quickly accumulate, and you need to be aware of them. Here is a small list of some of the fees associated with buying a home:

✓ First off, a **home appraisal** and a **home inspection** are not one in the same. The primary difference between home inspections and appraisals has to do with the goal or purpose. An appraisal seeks to determine the market value of the house, while the inspection is designed to evaluate the property's condition. Ask your lender how much they will charge to get an exact price you will have to pay the appraiser. You will want to know this price upfront. You will want to get a home inspector to expect the house you are interested in. Having the home inspected is a must. A certified inspector knows what to look for when it comes to finding hidden cosmetic cover-ups. Like holes in walls that have been recently patched and painted over. You do not want to second guess this process. I have witnessed so many people suffer dearly due to not having the home they are interested in inspected by a licensed home inspector. I will have questions for you at the end of this book that you should know the answers to before you purchase a home.

✓ You should get familiar with the term "**Closing Costs**." I promise you that you will be dealing with closing costs when buying a home. The term "closing costs" is a category that encompasses many distinct fees associated with closing on a home purchase. Here are some of the fees that may be associated with "closing costs." You may have (HOA) Homeowner's Association initiation fees, recording fees, pest inspection fees, and county and state taxes.

✓ Many times, at "closing," lenders will require you to put several months of mortgage insurance, property taxes, and property insurance payments in an **Escrow Account** at "closing." An escrow account is managed by a 3rd party where funds are held or accumulated until certain bills become due. I suggest that you set up an Escrow Account. If you are unfamiliar with Escrow Accounts and how they work, you will want to ask your home loan officer or loan originator how it works. Escrow Accounts help you stay on track with your taxes and insurance payments.

✓ Now that you know the difference between a home appraisal and an inspection, let's go over a **Home Inspection** in more detail. You are about to commit to spending hundreds of thousands to millions of dollars on a home. You owe it to yourself to have an in-depth home inspection conducted. You will want a certified, licensed home inspector who is affiliated with the American Society of Home Inspectors. Knowing your home is in great condition for such a significant investment will always be money well spent. I am sure you have heard the adage, "You can pay me now, or you can pay me later." This saying holds true. You can pay on the front end, or you can pay on the back end. Trust me! You will pay a whole lot more on the back end than on the front end.

✓ If you have plans to do something with your property after you have purchased it, you might want to take this section seriously. If you are looking to buy a condominium, that property might be part of a Homeowners Association or a Condominium Association that maintains the property's services and maintenance. These added services may include exterior landscaping, elevator maintenance, electricity, water, garbage, swimming pool, management office, and playground, among other things. You will want to know all of what the HOA covers and the associated monthly costs. There may also be a one-time setup fee charged at closing. You will need to look over the (**CC&R's**) **Covenants, Conditions, and Restrictions** guidelines in detail. If you are thinking about converting your property into an Airbnb, you might think again. Many condominium complexes are not allowing people to set up Airbnb. It is crucial that you find this out beforehand. Some condominium complexes don't even allow you to rent out your property. Once again, I will have questions listed at the end of the book that you will want to pay close attention to.

✓ You may want to set up an **emergency fund account**. Just because you have had a home inspection conducted, that does not mean that the home inspector will catch everything that may be wrong with the property or appliances. We all know that appliances can be in good condition one day and break down a day or a month later. Furthermore, some things like drywall, light fixtures, or windows may be damaged during the move-in process, so you may want to have an emergency fund account to take care of any emergencies that may unexpectedly come about when moving in.

✓ Let's talk about lender fees for a moment. This is one area of the home-buying process that most people find unappealing, but these fees need to be figured into the home-buying equation. I hate to be a bearer of bad news, but lenders do have fees. These fees can add up to a hefty amount. You will want to have your lender break down these fees. You will also want your lender to provide you with an estimate of fees before you sign any paperwork. Here is a list of various fees to expect: There will be Administration and document fees. Also, there will be escrow and filing fees. It is crucial that you do your homework.

✓ Now, let us talk about property tax. There will be a yearly tax paid to the county you reside in. Usually, the annual property tax is combined with your monthly mortgage payment. The lender will put your mortgage and tax payment into an escrow account until those bills come due. Taxes will vary from state to state and county to county. Refer to your county's real estate division and lender for costs associated with your potential home. One thing that may give you comfort in knowing is that the majority of your property tax payments will go to public schools and the maintenance of public roads, parks, and libraries.

✓ There is another tax that you should know about. Transfer tax is the tax associated with transferring the title from the seller to the buyer. It is comparable to sales tax on anything you might purchase from a store. Taxes will vary from state to state. You can always ask the closing agent and lender for state-specific taxes. For questions regarding the details and costs of your loan, refer to your county's real estate division, closing agent, or lender.

✓ You may have other various expenses connected to your home loan. There are other fees or costs associated with purchasing a home, like supplemental tax or utility bills, a community fee, or parking fees, to name a few. Keep in mind that each property is different. Make sure to ask the seller and agent to check for any costs associated with the property you have chosen to acquire.

CHAPTER SIX

KNOWING HOW CREDIT SCORES CAN AFFECT YOU

> To get something you never had,
> you must do something you never did.
> *- Dr. Mark L. Huddleston Ph.D.*

You must understand how your **credit scores** affect your interest rates. If you are not closely checking your credit scores, you should start now. The higher your credit scores, the lower your interest rate will be. When considering a thirty-year home loan for potentially hundreds of thousands of dollars, a quarter or half percent increase in your interest rate can cost tens of thousands of dollars in additional interest charges. **Credit scores** will range between 300 and 850. Lenders use these scores to determine how likely someone is to repay their loan. As you may already know, your credit score is calculated using your credit history. **The better your credit history, the higher your credit score.**

These are the three credit bureaus:

- ✓ Experian.
- ✓ Equifax.
- ✓ TransUnion.

Below is a table showing credit score brackets and the percentage of Americans in each.

16% have a credit score of	300 – 579	Which is very poor
18% have a credit score of	580 – 669	Which is fair
21% have a credit score of	670 – 739	Which is good
25% have a credit score of	740 – 799	Which is very good
20% have a credit score of	800 – 850	Which is exceptional

To find out where you stand regarding your credit score. There are websites like CreditKarma.com that offer wonderful tools for learning about your credit score, payment history, and insights on how to improve your credit score.

If you have always been debt-free or have no sources of building credit, you may discover that you may not have a credit score. While being debt-free is good, not having a credit score isn't all that great, and your mortgage options will be limited as a result.

If you are like the 34% of Americans with a credit score under 650, you will want to work on improving that score. On the other hand, you can find a lender who practices manual underwriting, which will help you get a mortgage without relying on a credit score. Churchill Mortgage is such a mortgage company that endorses this type of mortgage.

For the rest of us, here are some basic factors that may affect your credit score. You will want to pay close attention to them all:

You will want to be aware of your **payment history**. Late or missed payments are the most damaging factors when it comes to your credit scores. Just a few late payments can really ruin everything you worked so hard for. Apps like Bill Tracker or Mint.com can help you keep track of any outstanding financial obligations you may still have outstanding.

Making sure you pay on time is the first step to improving your credit score. Any debt collection accounts, like utility bills, old gym memberships, or library fees, can hurt you. If you have any outstanding expenses, pay them as soon as possible. Most lenders don't want to see any lates for at least two years.

Now many of us need to be aware of having **too much debt** and **too many credit accounts** open at the same time. Debt is a finely crafted concept that can enhance the quality of life immensely when leveraged correctly. Conversely, if you have too much debt, lenders will be hesitant to loan you more money, as this debt could overburden you. On the other hand, too little debt history will not show how responsible you are for completing your financial obligations.

My personal opinion would be to have as little debt as possible. Paying off your outstanding debt shows lenders that there is a good chance that you will pay back what you owe. The more accounts you open and pay off, the better your credit score will be. Having a credit card that you pay in full every month is a good way to build credit.

The age of your credit history is also very important. As I mentioned earlier in this chapter, the longer you can show on-time payments, the better. Having a long-standing credit history ranging from 5 to 10 years would be better than having only 1 to 2 years of credit history. This shows lenders that you have a steady financial foundation without much financial fluctuation. This will be important when a lender is evaluating your mortgage loan application.

You must be cognizant of **Hard Inquiries** in your credit report. Every time your credit is pulled by a lender, seller, or landlord to be reviewed, you're usually looking to obtain more credit. This can be anything from a car to an apartment or more credit cards. Lenders and underwriters will need to take a deep look at your credit history. When lenders and underwriters look at your credit history, that would be called an inquiry. When trying to obtain credit for a vehicle or home that would fall under the category of a Hard Inquiry. These hard inquiries will usually hurt your credit score for a short period of time. (3 to 6 months).

There is a way to soften these Hard Inquiries hits to your credit score. You will want to contact all three credit bureaus. I have supplied you with the addresses and phone numbers of those credit bureaus below. Once you contact them, you will want to inform them that you are car shopping or home shopping. You will want to give them a time frame of when you will be shopping. Many times, the credit bureaus will cut you some slack.

CREDIT REPORTING AGENCIES:

**Equifax Information
Services LLC**
P.O. Box 740241
Atlanta, GA 30374
1-800-685-1111

TransUnion Consumer Relations
2 Baldwin Place
P.O. Box 2000
Chester, PA 19022
1-800-916-8800

Experian, Inc.
Consumer Assistance
P.O. Box 2002
701 Experian Parkway
Allen, TX 75013-0036
1-888-397-3742

Early Warning Services, LLC
16552 N 90th Street Suite 100
Scottsdale, AZ 85260
1-800-204-4616

Next, I will cover the importance of **Credit Card Utilization**. Credit cards usually come with a limit on how much you can spend each month. If you are spending anything over 35% of that limit per month, you will be hurting your credit score. For example: Let's say your bank card has a $10,000 monthly limit. If you are spending more than $3,500 on that card, you will be negatively impacting your credit score. The rationale behind this is that even though you can spend up to $10,000 doesn't mean you should.

Not utilizing your full credit limit shows lenders how responsible you really are. A trick that could help is to call your credit card company about every six months and ask them to increase your credit limit. Getting your utilization down to 10% is how you'll start boosting your credit score. Another trick is to pay off as much of the credit card balance as you can before your statement is reported to the credit bureaus. This way, your low balance is what gets reported and counted toward your credit card utilization. You will want to call the credit card company and ask what time of the month they report to the credit bureaus. Keep in mind that all credit card companies do not report at the same time of the month.

The last thing you want to do is ignore potential inaccuracies in your credit report. They do happen, and you need to avoid them as much as possible. If you are regularly checking your credit report, you might notice some discrepancies or errors in your credit history. Someone with a similar name or social security number may have been coded to your credit file.

The credit bureaus: Experian, Equifax, and Transunion are required to investigate disputes that are submitted due to the **Fair Credit Reporting Act**. If you notice any errors, report them because they could have a negative impact on your credit score.

CHAPTER SEVEN

UNDERSTANDING THE VARIOUS TYPES OF MORTGAGES & INSURANCES

I would rather work with a person with
common sense than an educated idiot.
- Dr. Mark Huddleston Ph.D.

You will want to do research on the different types of mortgages after getting your financial credit reports in order. You should have a better idea of how much your monthly payments are going to be, but you still need to understand the various types of mortgages and select which one you want. Your loan officer will present several different options on how to structure your loan. Normally, there are four types of mortgages to choose from:

- ✓ Conventional
- ✓ Government-insured
- ✓ Adjustable-rate mortgages (ARM)

✓ Sharia-compliant mortgages

Let me define what a conventional mortgage is: There are two different forms of conventional (or fixed) mortgages. These are known as conforming and non-conforming loans. A conforming loan classifies your loan amount under the limits set forth by Fannie Mae or Freddie Mac: For those who don't know, Fannie Mae or Freddie Mac were created by Congress to provide liquidity, stability, and affordability to the mortgage market. If your loan exceeds those limits, it is classified as non-conforming.

Conventional loans are the most common since they can be used for primary, vacation, and investment properties. Buyers making down payments of less than 20% will be required to pay **primary mortgage insurance** (**PMI**). PMI usually costs anywhere between 0.5 % to 1.0% of the loan amount annually. As an example, if you buy a $500,000 home and put $50,000 down (10%), your loan balance would be $450,000. PMI costs will range between $2,250 to $4,500 per year or $187.50 to $375.00 per month.

What are the advantages of Conventional Mortgages:

✓ The total cost involved with borrowing is typically lower. This holds true even when interest rates might be above average.

✓ If your down payment was less than 20%, you could request your lender to eliminate PMI once you have accrued 20% equity.

✓ Certain government-back loans allow you to pay as little as 3% down.

What are the disadvantages of Conventional Mortgages:

✓ Prepare yourself for a lengthy documentation process that will verify income, assets, down payment, and employment.

✓ Your credit score needs to be higher than 620.

✓ Your credit history must show a debt-to-income ratio between 45% to 50%.

✓ In the case that your down payment is lower than 20%, you will most likely be required to pay PMI.

What types of people should get a conventional mortgage?

Anyone buying a home that doesn't qualify for a government-sponsored loan should consider a conventional mortgage. Whether you've missed payments, have too much debt, or don't have enough credit history, you may be one of the many Americans with a credit score of less than 620. As discussed earlier, you should first focus on improving your credit score by paying off small debts or <u>acquiring</u> <u>an</u> <u>authorized</u> <u>tradeline</u>. The other way to pay down debt is to apply snowballing or debt stacking. As illustrated in my other book, "**The Essential Keys To Financial Freedom**." Snowballing and Debt Stacking are great methods for paying down debt and should be considered if you are inundated by bills and mounting debt.

If your debt-to-income ratio is greater than 45%, you need to focus on reducing that percentage. Banks will look at your application more favorably if you can show a history of paying your debts on time. The idea is to be financially stable before buying your home. Lenders don't want to see that your mortgage payments will put you in financial instability. If paying off debt isn't helping your credit score, find a lender who practices manual underwriting. This lender can help you get a mortgage without relying on a credit score. Additionally, if you can put 20 % down to avoid PMI, do it.

Government-insured mortgages

The U.S. government likes to see people buy homes. They benefit from people purchasing properties. In addition to the many tax benefits, there are also three government institutions that back home loans. Those agencies are the **Federal Housing Administration** (FHA), the **U.S. Department of Agriculture** (USDA), and the **U.S. Department of Veterans Affairs** (VA).

FHA Loans

The Federal Housing Administration provides prospective buyers without a 20% down payment and with less-than-perfect credit, the opportunity to become homeowners. With a credit score of 580 or above, FHA loans allow you to put down as little as 3.5%. In the event your credit score is under 580, you can still qualify for an FHA loan, but you must put down at least 10% and have a credit score over 500.

However, putting down less than 10%, FHA loans stipulate that they must obtain two mortgage insurance premiums, the first due before closing on the property and the second an annual payment that lasts for the life of the loan.

USDA Loans

Do you live in a rural area? Is your county or town's population less than 10,000? If so, you may be interested in a USDA loan. The USDA provides loans to low-income individuals seeking to purchase a home in a rural area. Now in order to qualify, your home must be located in a USDA-eligible area. According to the guidelines set by the USDA, an area is considered rural if the population is less than 10,000 people. Additionally, your income must be under a certain limit to be eligible for the loan. You may or may not be required to pay a down payment for a USDA loan. This varies from region to region. If you meet the location and income requirements, USDA loans are a great way to find mortgage credit in areas where a lack of opportunity exists.

VA Loans

Veterans of the United States military and their immediate family members can acquire loans backed by the VA. This type of loan represents an incredibly flexible, low-interest rate option that many veterans can take advantage of. The biggest advantages of a VA loan are its low-down payment, lack of PMI, and capped closing costs. VA loan borrowers will need to cover a funding fee, which is a set percentage of the loan amount. The funding fee and other minimized closing costs can all be taken care of upfront or included on the back end of your loan.

Advantages of Government-Insured Loans

✓ Both first-time buyers and repeat homeowners can qualify.
✓ FICO score minimums are not as high as conventional limits.
✓ Down payments are often lower, allowing individuals with small down payments the ability to purchase.

Disadvantages of Government-Insured Loans

✓ The documentation process can be demanding.
✓ Qualification requirements are strict.
✓ Obligatory mortgage insurance premiums are unavoidable.
✓ The cost of closing the loan may be higher than conventional loans.

Who should get a government-insured loan?

Obtaining a mortgage backed by the federal government can feel like a true blessing. The favorable terms make the process much easier than obtaining conventional loans. If you don't have a large amount of cash saved or suffer from bad credit marks on your credit file, you may want to consider a government-insured loan. Out of the different types, VA loans are the most borrower-friendly and are used as an advantage or selling point for recruiters in the military. To that end, USDA loans and FHA loans offer the rest of the populace a great alternative to the stricter requirements that come along with conventional loans.

Adjustable-Rate Mortgages (ARMs)

It is my personal opinion that obtaining an adjustable-rate loan is like gambling. Let me go into more detail. How is the market performing? What are interest rates like? Do you feel like you can pay off the loan before the market shifts? These are all questions you will want to consider before getting into an adjustable-rate mortgage. The name says it all. ARMs have a shifting interest rate that adjusts according to the market.

Typically, lenders offer ARMs with a fixed rate for the first twelve or twenty-four months that is lower than a conventional loan. You must be careful not to fall for this so-called "sucker rate" because, after the specified period, the loan will adjust itself according to the market for the remainder of the term. You want to be mindful and secure an ARM that has a limit or cap on how much the interest rate or mortgage payment can increase. The last thing you want to see is your payment go from $1,200 to $3,200 overnight.

I know many of you want to know **the advantages of adjustable-rate mortgages**. Just to be clear, the first few years of your adjustable-rate mortgage may be locked in at a lower rate than a conventional loan. It is also possible to significantly cut down your interest payments with an adjustable-rate mortgage.

There are also **disadvantages to adjustable-rate mortgages**. There is a possibility that your monthly mortgage payments can double or even triple. Adjustable-rate mortgages have high loan default rates. Lastly, your financial freedom may be tied to how stable the market is. This is why I am not a fan of adjustable-rate mortgages. Once again, that is just my opinion.

I am sure you are wondering who should get an adjustable-rate mortgage. Characteristically, buyers who feel extremely confident in their ability to pay off the adjustable-rate mortgage before it adjusts should get one. It's my personal recommendation to avoid an adjustable-rate mortgage period. Because you never know what can happen to the economy. There could be a major shift in the market that can affect your monthly mortgage payment immensely. This is the number one reason adjustable-rate mortgages have higher than average default rates.

I just covered the major mortgage types available in the United States. Regardless of the mortgage you choose, you can use an online calculator to help estimate your mortgage payment, or you can have a loan officer or loan originator help you figure this out. I recommend visiting MortgageCalculator.org or Zillow.com/Mortgage-Calculator. You will want to have the following information with you when you visit these websites:

- ✓ Down Payment.
- ✓ HOA Fees.
- ✓ Home insurance.
- ✓ Interest Rate.
- ✓ PMI.
- ✓ Purchase price.
- ✓ Real Estate Tax.

I recommend that you verify that there are no prepayment penalties. What I mean by this is that you don't want to get penalized for paying off your mortgage loan early. You don't want to get stuck paying any additional fees.

I hope you are following all that I have shared with you. Once again, I recommend that you talk to a licensed loan officer and a certified financial advisor. Talking to a licensed loan officer and certified financial advisor will help bring to your attention any details you may have overlooked. Please be honest about your financial situation and provide accurate financial documents, such as bank statements, tax returns, bills, etc., to your loan officer and financial advisor. After reviewing your financial documents, a good loan officer and financial advisor will help expand your knowledge of what you can afford, how much to put down, and what additional fees to expect when buying your home.

Your loan officer will be a wonderful resource when trying to make important financial decisions regarding your loan and let you know what you might qualify for. Getting pre-qualified is a quick calculation the loan officer will do to give you a sense of the types of loans and the amount you may be approved for based on the high-level information you provide. You must understand that it is not a commitment and is for informational purposes only.

The next step is to get pre-approved for a loan. The pre-approval process requires you to complete an application that gives the lender a better understanding of your financial situation as well as verify some information via a background check or credit check. If everything checks out with the application, they will be able to provide you with preliminary financing approval, as well as an expectation of what rate you can expect. This will be your preapproval letter when submitting an offer on a home.

Although the preapproval letter is not a binding commitment, it is typically good for a minimum of 90 days and a maximum of 180 days so that you don't need to complete another application, background check, or credit check in that time frame.

CHAPTER EIGHT
LOOKING FOR THE IDEAL HOME

I am a believer that how you do anything is
how you do everything.
- *Dr. Mark L. Huddleston Ph.D.*

A ll right! You have made major progress. It is time for you
to look for the ideal home. I know you have heard of
the adage "home sweet home." Buying your very own home is
one of the greatest feelings and one of the best investments a
person can make. A home is where you feel safe. Your personal
sanctuary. A place where you can totally relax and unwind after
a long stressful day, either by yourself or with your family or
loved ones.

A home serves many key purposes, so it's important that
you find the most suitable home for yourself. Performing proper
due diligence on a property before buying is more of an obligation than a recommendation. In this chapter, I will cover some
crucial considerations you must not overlook when buying
your home.

At this juncture, you will want to interview Real Estate Agents or Real Estate Brokers. Let me be the first to tell you that real estate agents and brokers are not created equal. So, you will want to take what I am about to share with you seriously. Your decision at this point can make or break you.

First of all, know that a Real Estate Broker is someone who has gone beyond the scope necessary to become a real estate agent to obtain their state real estate broker license. A broker is different from an agent as they can work independently. Start their own brokerage and/or hire other real estate agents.

Brokers, in most cases, have more knowledge than ordinary agents. I personally work with real estate brokers. If you do decide to work with an agent, you will want to interview several agents. Some agents are knowledgeable and will go the extra mile, and some agents aren't. You will not want to rush this process.

Interviewing and picking the best real estate agent is one of the most important steps you can take before your home search process. Among all the excitement of looking for your dream home, it can be easy to skip crucial steps needed to secure the perfect home, but there's no reason not to use a real estate agent or broker. First of all, they can provide vital feedback and guidance throughout your home search.

Keep in mind that the seller of the home typically pays the commission for both the buyer and seller's agent, but if you're in a market where the seller does not pay the buyer broker commission, it's still a great idea to hire an agent or broker of your own.

Conversely, you won't have to pay a single penny to have an agent or broker represent you and help you find the perfect home. Why not have someone knowledgeable in the real estate market advise you free of charge? Purchasing a home is the most important financial commitment most people will ever make. Receiving the best advice and counseling possible is crucial. Just because you are not paying the agent or broker directly doesn't mean you should settle for any old agent or broker.

Many times, I have seen agents and brokers alike push their clients to buy or sell a home just to make a commission. I've seen countless individuals willing to invest their hard-earned money in expensive homes with a mediocre agent or broker with little or no experience or credibility. I would not recommend this route at all.

Whatever you do, don't choose a broker or agent simply because they are a family member or friend. You will want to interview several agents or brokers and pick the one that is the most knowledgeable about the location, price range, and style of the type of home for which you are looking for. You will want to ask to see their portfolio of what they have helped buy or sell.

I can't tell you enough, make sure you choose the right agent or broker, and don't settle for just anyone. Here is a list of characteristics you should seek in a great agent or broker:

✓ You will want to find an agent or broker **who is knowledgeable**. If an agent or broker is knowledgeable, they will most likely have plenty of resources at their disposal to help assist you. Your agent or broker should be able to speak about all facets of the home-buying process. I don't want to sound redundant, but this is very important. **Here are a few areas in which your agent or broker should be an expert in.**

✓ Look for an agent or broker who is currently active in the real estate market. Someone who is presently buying and selling for clients would be perfect. This type of agent or broker will have a feel and **understanding of the market**. Like anything else, trends and fads come and go. Understanding where the market is currently will help you buy smarter.

The next characteristic that should not go without mentioning is making sure that the agent or broker you choose understands the type of area you would like to reside in. It comes down to location. You will want to find an agent or broker that understands the community they serve. If you want to live in region A and your agent or broker is only familiar with regions B and C, they will not be of much help to you. You will want an expert touch of familiarity, local knowledge, and honesty. This describes the agent or broker you want to work with.

Agents and brokers, in many cases, typically stick to a **specific home type or style**. Some specialize in high price mansions, some focus on plots of land, and others specialize in farms and ranches. I think you get the idea. Just make sure your agent or broker is familiar with the type of home that you are looking for. For example, if you are trying to find affordable townhouses, you don't want to work with an agent or broker whose portfolio is filled with extravagant condominiums.

This next section may not be important to you but is very important to me. An agent or broker that understands the quality and variety of construction materials will do you a world of good. They will be able to help you acquire the right home for you. Many experienced agents and brokers will be able to look at a home and know what type of construction materials were used when built. They will investigate when the home was built, what person or company constructed it and designed the home and know its long-term value. To know all this will take an experienced agent or broker to gather all the pertinent information. A knowledgeable agent or broker will also be able to point out how well or poorly constructed a property is. An agent or broker doing this will help you understand the long-term maintenance costs if you were to purchase the property.

Agents and brokers are not lawyers. This is why I personally work with brokers. They have more schooling than ordinary agents. Please don't take me wrong. There are good agents out there. I was only stating my preference. You will need an agent or broker to walk you through a contract and explain some key elements you will need to know to close the real estate transaction. Just know that real estate law and contracts can be confusing and complicated. With complicated financing terms, numerous parties, strict closing requirements, and other variables, you will need an agent or broker who can explain it all in easy and understandable terms and articulate those terms in a way that it is clear and to the point.

I am a true believer in backup plans. A **contingency clause** can help protect (you) the buyer in the event an item in the contract is not satisfactorily fulfilled. Here is an example of what I mean. A financing contingency gives the buyer an out if they are not able to ensure the funds for closing. Working out the logistics of your contingency plan with your agent or broker is a must. Having a contingency plan can save the day if all fails.

Let's go over mortgages a little more. It matters whom you have your mortgage with. A good agent or broker can steer you to a good **mortgage broker** if you can't find one that will represent you. A good mortgage broker can guide you through the various options to guarantee that you obtain the best rate and loan setup. Having a second set of eyes can always help when looking over your mortgage paperwork. If you can't find a decent mortgage loan officer, your agent or broker should be able to direct you to one. As I mentioned earlier in this book. Having a mortgage loan officer is a must. They specialize in home loans. If you have any questions about mortgages that your agent or broker can't answer, a loan officer should be able to answer them for you.

Having a good agent or broker is invaluable. They can review your settlement statement and correct any mistakes or discrepancies. In addition to that, your agent or broker can walk you through everything you sign at closing. Who can ask for more?

What I value most in an agent or broker would be **honesty**. True honesty is few and far between. Honesty is everything. You want an agent or broker who will be looking out for your best interests. Buying a home can be a very stressful time in a buyer's life. Having an agent or broker ready to expose potential problems is crucial. Whether it be financial, market-based, or regarding the house itself, a good agent or broker will help you steer clear of common pitfalls. Your agent or broker should be willing to put your interests before their own. Actually, it is the agent or broker's fiduciary responsibility to look out for their client's best interests.

Communication between you and your agent or broker can make the difference in you getting what you want in a home. Most problems stem from real estate agents and brokers not being able to communicate well with their clients. You want to make sure that you find an agent or broker that has the ability to listen to what your wants, needs, and desires are when it comes to what you want. It is important that you are working with an agent or broker that can effectively and consistently articulate information. Always remember that communication goes both ways.

When you decide on what agent or broker you will be working with, you will want to make a list of the wants and needs you are looking for so the agent or broker can tailor their efforts appropriately. If you explicitly state you need a two-car garage, and your agent or broker keeps showing you homes with one garage, you have a problem. It could be that a two-car garage home is out of your price range, but if you drive the extra mile, you will find plenty of two-car garage homes. You must be clear about your expectations and mean what you say and say what you mean.

If you are like many people, you will look to see what people have to say about services they have used in the past. I would recommend that you do the same when looking for an agent or broker. Why not **get recent references** from the agent or broker you are interested in representing you? If an agent or broker has an online presence, you will want to review some of those **references**. Ask the agent or broker about the past five sales they have made. This will help determine if you are talking to the right agent or broker to see if they have the appropriate skills to help you with purchasing a home.

Once you have selected the agent or broker you are happy with, you will then sign a buyer broker and agency agreement, which will validate your relationship with the agent or broker you have chosen to work with. It also establishes the agent or broker's fiduciary responsibility to you as the buyer.

You can sign an **exclusive agreement** that obligates you to use that agent or broker exclusively. The advantage of having an exclusive agreement is to show the agent or broker just how serious you are and how committed you are to them. The agent or broker you have chosen to work with will be more attentive to your wants and needs. Signing a **nonexclusive agreement** with your agent or broker allows you to work with all agents. The upside to signing a nonexclusive agreement is that you may receive information and listings from several agents. No matter if you choose an exclusive or a nonexclusive agreement, make sure your agreement has a termination option for any reason so that you are not stuck with a nonproductive agent or broker for a long period of time.

Please open your mind to what I'm about to share with you. Searching for a home within your budget is key to buying your first home. Not staying within your budget is one of the main reasons why most people who buy a home lose their home. The key here is to own your home instead of the home owning you.

You can save time by narrowing your search to homes that fit your financial requirements. You will want to stick within the budget, you and your home loan officer come up with. Being realistic about what you can afford, where you are in life, and what you truly need is vital.

I get it! We all want an 8-bedroom house with a 4-car garage, on a hill overlooking the city, with a swimming pool and pool house, with maid quarters, on 10 acres of land. Let's get real. I know we watch TV and see movie stars living in those large luxury homes and driving those fancy cars and dream about living that way ourselves. I know this philosophy runs deep within our society, and we may feel social pressures to purchase items we cannot afford. We all want to keep up with the Jones and don't realize that the Jones are living a lie.

This mentality causes many of us to accumulate vast amounts of debt. By following the steps, I have listed in this book, you will be able to determine what you can afford. Look for only the homes that fit your financial needs instead of trying to fake it until you make it. You must filter out those elaborate homes outside of your price range. You will save a lot of time, effort, and heartache by staying within your budget.

In this next section, many people may not agree with me when it comes to previewing properties online. I get it! We live in a time where almost everything we want is just a click away, including property searches. After several searches, filters, and clicks, you will find every home type in every location, price range, and criteria you have specified.

You can use websites like ZipRealty, Zillow, or Redfin, just to name a few, to give you an idea of the estimated value, market trends, and neighborhood details of your potential home. Keep in mind that these tools help consolidate what's on the market that might be of interest to you. Viewing photos and taking virtual tours can assist you in identifying what your preferences are. While these tools can be helpful, in many cases, the information about the home is not accurate. You must read the fine print. On many occasions, these sites often provide a disclaimer: "Information on this site does not provide financial or real estate advice and may not be accurate." They also may not take into consideration the specific terms the sellers are willing to offer or renovations that may have added significant value to the property.

On occasion, buyers will send me pictures of homes that are in their price range and want to know my opinion. First of all, I look deeper than the average buyer. I make it a point to go look at a property firsthand. Pictures can be doctored up with cosmetic overlays. Many times, foundation fractures can't be seen in pictures. Dry rot can be painted over. Flood damage can be concealed as well. Pest problems, like cockroaches, termites, silverfish, and rodents, won't be photographed by the seller. Roof leaks will be covered up and painted over. **This is**

the main reason why most sellers put their homes on the market during the summer months. I also look to see if any mechanical liens have been placed on the property. I make sure to see if the property is up to code.

When buyers ask for my opinion, the first thing I do is go to the website where the buyer found the proposed property. I look at the website description to see if it is missing the association fee, which may push the property outside of the monthly payment of the buyer's budget. Sometimes, a brand-new home will show a price drop of $50,000 online, and eager home buyers are quick to jump at this opportunity. Many times, after investigating, the listing is just pulling the same address for both the 2,400 square foot unit and the 3,200 square foot unit the builder is selling.

As I have stated many times throughout this book already, you must do your homework and send properties that interest you to your agent or broker to get their feedback. Let them review all the information and verify whether it's a good fit for you. Make sure your agent or broker can validate important information like HOA fees, taxes, or any other restrictions. You want your agent or broker to understand all the details before they pull the trigger. You may want to ask your agent or broker to take a look at the proposed property at night-time. The reason for this is that most neighborhoods that have drug and crime activity usually takes place at sundown.

A short while ago, I had a seller ask me how much they thought they could list their condo for sale. After researching the market and walking through their twenty-five-year-old home, I told them they would get the most value if they were willing to do some slight renovations for around $15,000. I informed them if they were not willing to do so that, they could possibly sell their property for $360,000.

The seller told me my information must be wrong because their neighbors had their condo listed for $399,990. After the seller informed me of that listing, I suggested that we take a look at their neighbor's condo. Their neighbor's condo was fully renovated with brand-new stainless-steel kitchen appliances, granite countertops, and hardwood floors. Their neighbor's home was immaculate. (Top Shelf)! The sellers immediately understood what I meant and renovated their home over the next month for just under $15,000. When renovations were all completed, their home sold for $405,000 a week later.

Previewing properties online can be very helpful, but a good agent or broker will be able to see past the cosmetics and find the truth for you.

It is just my opinion that **you should visit your preselected properties in person**. After selecting 5 to 8 properties that fit your wants, needs, and desires and are within your budget, it will be time to go take a closer look at those properties. **I can't stress this enough. Never purchase a property without viewing it in person**.

Know that no two homes are the same and every single home is unique, even if they're in the same community and have the same layout. Buying a home is unlike any other purchase you will ever make. Let's take buying a new motorcycle as an example. You could be living in Florida but find a new or used motorcycle at a dealer in California that you want to purchase. It would make total sense to visit your local dealership and test-drive the same type and style of motorcycle. You can get a list of all the options from the motorcycle Vehicle Identification Number on the California motorcycle.

After researching all the specs of the motorcycle, you are interested in. If the motorcycle is right for you, just call the dealer in California and purchase the motorcycle, knowing you will have a full factory warranty on defective parts. The risk is minimal.

Buying a home is much different from buying a motorcycle. First of all, there is probably no home built to the exact same specifications as yours. There might be similarities in floor plans, but the property's location, options, materials, and finishes will be immensely different. When I state location, I don't just mean miles apart. Even homes in the same neighborhood won't be identical. One home could be facing the south with all the windows on the north side. Good luck getting any natural light in that section of the house. Another home could be right next to a main street with the sounds of cars, along with seeing the lights from those cars passing by your living room every three seconds. But maybe the third home is perfect for you.

This is why viewing a home in person is essential. In the end, you will spend a considerable amount of time living in it. Pictures won't be accurate in portraying the property's size, dimensions, layout, or surroundings. You will want to get a feel for the home, and the only way to do that is to visit that home in person.

Once you've found the house you want to call home sweet home, it will be time to make an intelligent and informed offer; you need to do your research. Check out the sales prices on comparable properties in the neighborhood over the past year. What pros and cons does your potential home have compared to those that have recently sold? How many days has the home been on the market? What is the pricing history? In the next chapter, I will cover what to do with all the information you have uncovered before you make an offer on the property you have targeted.

CHAPTER NINE
MAKING AN INFORMED OFFER

You don't wait for an opportunity; you create one!
- Dr. Mark L. Huddleston Ph.D.

Now that you've made headway, it is time to make an informed offer on the home you're interested in. Optimistically, if everything goes smoothly, you will be relaxing in your new home, pondering over this entire process. Before all of this can happen, you, your agent, or your broker have to negotiate the best agreement possible. This will include much more than the best purchase price. Your offer must be a knowledgeable one, so you can back up your negotiation with satisfactory points.

Making a good offer is about finding a balance between what you can afford, getting the most property for your dollar, and submitting an offer the seller is willing to accept. You also need to be mindful of timing, financing, and added costs, among other things. As stated in a national report, approximately 15% of homeowners said that it was thought-provoking to have the seller accept their initial offer on the home they were interested in. Keep in mind that there is a lot to consider, like getting your offer accepted can be easily accomplished if you consider and answer the following questions first:

- ✓ What's the seller's timeline? What's your timeline?
- ✓ What's the market value of the home you are interested in?
- ✓ What's the seller's list price?
- ✓ What incentives is the seller offering?
- ✓ How are market conditions now?
- ✓ How competitive is the submarket?
- ✓ Is it a buyer's market? Or a seller's market?
- ✓ How much can you afford for your monthly payment?
- ✓ How much are the extra costs? And what do they cover?
- ✓ What are the home's features?
- ✓ How much additional work does the home require?

Don't let these questions frighten you. Your agent or broker should know these questions by heart, and if they don't, you should have these questions available to present to them.

Let's start with the **home type**. Home types include townhouses, condominiums, and single-family homes. Certain home types, such as condos, may come with additional restrictions or costs, such as condo dues or homeowner association fees.

What is the **home size**? What is the square footage of the home? I promise you that this question will become an issue when negotiating the price. So, make sure you know it.

What is the **lot size**? How much land does the home sit on? Are there any restrictions or codes that need to be brought up to date? A simple title survey should give you all the information you require.

How many bedrooms does the home have? And how many of those rooms can be added to if needed? **To be considered a bedroom, you need to have a window, closet, and smoke detector installed.** This is a very important point to cover with your agent or broker before making an offer. Just a suggestion. You can always convert your garage into a bedroom or two. Just something to think about.

How many bathrooms does the home have? Don't confuse a washroom with a full bathroom. If the room does not have a shower or bathtub, it would be considered a washroom.

Exterior and **interior features** can bring much value to the home you are interested in. You will need to find out if any of the home appliances are included. Do curtains or blinds come with the home? This also includes other supplemental features you may be interested in, like fireplaces, light fixtures, tubs, upgraded cabinets, or quartz versus granite or laminate countertops. Are the floors hardwood, tile, vinyl, or carpet? Is there anything that requires immediate attention? Are there any additional purchases you will have to make? These are all minor costs that can quickly add up.

Does your home come with any kind of storage? **Do you pay for the utilities?** Who pays for the heating, cooling, gas, and electricity, you or the H.O.A.? Do not make an offer before you find out what the utility costs will amount to. Know that properties that do not have public utilities such as natural gas or public water and sewer can have higher maintenance or usage costs than the average home.

Let us not forget about **parking**. Is there a garage or number of assigned parking spaces for the buyer? Is there enough public parking for you and your guests? Is the driveway space large enough for your family's needs? The reason why I am bringing this point up is due to so many buyers complaining about being charged for having too many vehicles and getting fined for having more than the acceptable number of vehicles permitted on the property.

As I mentioned earlier in this book, it is vital that you identify **what year your potential home was built**. The older the home is, the more maintenance it will probably require. As I mentioned before, you will want to find out if the home you are interested in is up to (code). Many times, an older home will not be up to city or state zoning codes. What I mean by this is, if your home does not have sidewalks in front of it when you buy the home, you may be responsible for putting sidewalks in front of your home. Owners of older homes may be grandfathered in, meaning that there was no code to put sidewalks in when the previous owner bought the home. Staying on top of these repairs and city and state zoning codes will save you money in the long run. Additionally, wear and tear items like heating or air-conditioning units, windows, and roofs, typically don't add value to the home when replaced but rather keep it up to market standards. You will want to keep all of this in mind when a seller begins explaining all the items that have been recently renovated.

Next, you will want to do some **comparative home analyzing**. This will only give you an idea of how the market is performing. This does not give you the final word. I have seen properties that are similar go for different prices. One property sold for $278,000, and a similar property, in the same complex went for a whopping $480,000. What it all comes down to is what a buyer is willing to pay.

Once you have answered the previous questions mentioned in this chapter, you will be able to consider the total cost of homeownership and make a well-informed offer. A great way to congruently answer these questions would be to **create a property cheat sheet** or **information sheet**. This list should have the seller's list price, incentives, home features, and the extra costs associated with the property. Any information you don't have on hand can be found in the listing or in public records. When in doubt, you can always ask your agent or broker to earn their commission by gathering this information.

You may want to take it a step further and ask your agent or broker to create a **Comparative Market Analysis (CMA)**. A Comparative Market Analysis is a helpful way to understand the home's market value and current market conditions. As I stated earlier, no two homes are exactly alike. Therefore, it's incredibly difficult to utilize an apple-to-apple approach when trying to find your future home's market value.

It is essential to analyze the details of similar homes to make a measurable assumption on your potential home value. I have listed some metrics you should consider when constructing your Comparative Market Analysis:

- ✓ You will want to know what homes in the neighborhood, city, or county are selling for.
- ✓ How many houses are for sale?

Here is an example of what I mean: If there are two condos in a five-mile radius priced under $350,000, the demand may outweigh the supply, and therefore, you may need to move quickly. But, if there are eighty new condos in the same area, you will have more buying power and be able to be more selective or offer a lower price. Consider how competitive the home is priced, based on the home's features, compared with other available homes on the market.

On the other hand, look at similar homes that have sold in that same area. Look at your Comparative Market Analysis to see what comparable homes have sold in the past twelve months. Based on those comparisons and sales dates, you may be able to view specific trends like price increases, fewer days on the market, etc. These trends will help you analyze and determine what your offer should entail.

Since you have compiled a list of homes that have sold in the past twelve months, it is now time to use it. A good practice that I recommend in making a strong offer is checking both the **list price** and the **selling price**. This statistic will help you understand how much wiggle room you must negotiate and how to make a firm offer.

Next, you will want to find out how many days the home you have in your sights has been on the market. How many days, on average, are homes in the community on the market? The number of **days** a house has been **on** the **market** is a significant statistic to know. Most prospective buyers, realtors, and even real estate investors, in many cases, will associate a house with a high (**DOM**) as being undesirable. There must be a reason the house is not selling, right?

Some buyers may think the house has costly issues that need to be repaired. It could just be that the selling price is too high. A smart buyer will leverage this issue and negotiate the best price possible. If a home has been on the market for a significant amount of time, the seller will be more receptive to negotiations.

Sometimes, the motivation to sell is enough to save you thousands of dollars. Sellers are usually selling in order to move on to a new chapter of their lives and are probably aiming to sell by a specific date. If the home is vacant, they'll have carrying costs, such as a mortgage, utilities, etc., that accrue daily. The longer the house is on the market, the more likely you'll be able to negotiate a better price.

Now that you have consulted with your agent or broker and the two have answered all the questions that need to be answered, you should have a good idea of the price and terms you are going to offer the seller. Up to this point, **you should have adequately analyzed the home's features**, **prepared your financial budget**, and **considered added costs**. You should feel confident about moving forward.

I hope that everything I have conveyed to you thus far makes sense. My goal is to break the entire home-buying process down to the simplest terms possible.

The next step is to draft an offer with a written **Purchase** and **Sale Agreement** (**PSA**). The best way to do this is to use your state's standard approved template. State standard templates are a convenient way of guaranteeing you have a comprehensive PSA that includes all state-required legal language and laws.

You will want to take what I am about to share with you quite seriously. Just know that **cheaper is not always better, and better is not always cheaper**! If you draft your own (PSA) from scratch, you could incur legal fees as well as potentially miss some critical pieces of information that can come back to bite you on your a$$ in the future.

There are standard templates that are properly formatted to allow for fill-in-the-blank answers and have little check mark boxes to select the appropriate circumstances behind the scenario you have selected. I recommend that you sit down with an attorney who specializes in real estate matters to have them review or fill it in for you. Just know that **if you got it together, you don't have to get it together.**

Important note: It is imperative that you make sure you have the following information completed correctly:

You will want to sit down with your agent or broker and have them obtain the **address** and **legal property description information**. This information can be found in your county's public property records. Once again, your agent or broker should be able to provide this information to you as well. **Make your agent or broker earn their commission.**

You will want to have **the buyer's and seller's contact information**. Names are an evident requirement. Furthermore, having information like forwarding addresses or emails can help you receive essential documents during closing proceedings and post-proceedings of the real estate transaction.

You will want to ask your agent or broker if they know of any entity that gives **closing cost assistance**. I cannot stress this point enough. You can also go online and find first-time buyer programs that may be available to you in your state. When I purchased my first home, I used a charity that paid my down payment costs and all my closing costs. The agent that was assisting me in the transaction had no clue that there were first-time buyer programs available to me. I found that charity by browsing online myself.

I recommend that you ask for a percentage of your offer to be allocated to **closing cost assistance** if you are not successful in finding a charity to help with the down payment or closing costs. By asking for closing costs assistance, will ultimately save you from spending money toward closing costs and let you focus on putting more money down toward your principal, thus lowering your interest payments in the long term.

My recommendation to buyers is to negotiate closing cost assistance more than the sales price. In effect, you are reducing the sales price by 2 to 4 percent and saving thousands in interest payments that you would have paid if not doing so.

Next, you will want to present the seller with an **Earnest Money Deposit (EMD)**. This is also known as a security deposit or, in other terms, a good faith payment. This payment shows the buyer that you are serious about buying their home. Know when putting down an (EMD), that it is refundable until contingencies are waived. Once again, this is a wonderful way to prove to the buyer that you are serious about buying the property. Depending on your market standard, the (EMD) could be as little as $1,000 or as high as 5% of the purchase price.

You will want to protect what you are about to buy. As I mentioned earlier in this book. In most cases, buying a home will be the largest investment a person will ever make. So, you should do your due diligence to protect your investment at all costs. Unless you are buying a brand-new home from a builder, it would be a good idea to ask for **a home warranty**, paid for by the seller for the first year of ownership. Because you never know what could happen. The warranty would be provided by a third party, and depending on the package chosen, the warranty would cover anything from appliances to the integrity of the home's structure.

In the event you are buying a new home, it might give you some peace of mind to know that builders typically offer a warranty for the first year of ownership. Make sure you ask the builder for their specific warranty conditions.

You, your agent, or your broker must keep up with the **legal requirements** for the state you live in or desire to live in. Each state has different legal requirements and disclosures. Real estate law can be downright confusing. By using up-to-date, state-approved contracts will prevent future complications and/or issues, especially in unfortunate circumstances if litigation is necessary.

Next, I found out the hard way about **personal property** and **fixtures**. The story I am about to share with you is something I experienced when I bought my first home. You will want to make sure to specify what is being communicated. Find out what items are staying and what items the seller is going to take with them when the house is sold. Like, what appliances, light fixtures, curtains, etc.). I recommend that you make a list of this agreement and have the seller and you sign this agreement to avoid confusion at closing.

I don't want to come across as redundant, but I went through a rough time with the seller at closing because of this happening to me. The seller stated that they were leaving the refrigerator, light fixtures, and dishwasher. To my surprise, when moving into the home, all the light fixtures, dishwasher, and refrigerator were missing. To cut to the chase, I had to take the seller to court, where I ended up winning the legal battle and getting all the items returned and $10,000 to boot. The point I am trying to make is that you should dot all your I's and cross all your T's when conducting business transactions. Think about all the time I spent in court fighting this. I could think of a hundred things I would rather be doing than sitting in court over something as petty as what happened to me.

You will want to **know the price of the home**. You should share with the seller how much and how you will be paying for the home. You will also want to include any amount you plan on borrowing. For example: (25% down with a 75% loan).

Next, the buyer (you) gets to select whom they want to use as the **settlement agent**. The settlement agent is basically a middleman who collects funds from the buyer and ensures the seller pays any outstanding lenders, contractors, taxes, lien holders, etc., before providing you with the property title. For example, your earnest money deposit (EMD) would be sent to the settlement agent, who would hold the funds in an escrow account until everything has been investigated and settled.

The day you close on the intended property is known as the **settlement date**. You will want to give yourself enough time to take care of all unforeseen events that may arise. On average, the settlement date should be 30 to 45 days after the contract approval.

Once all the items have been covered and completed in your contract, you will want to verify that you have the **appropriate contingencies** and **supporting addendums**. The world we live in is filled with an excessive amount of uncertainty. Real estate is filled with hypothetical what-ifs and one-offs that can lead a person astray.

For example: What if the shower drains you just repaired burst again? What happens if the seller doesn't want to go through with closing? What if the bank delivers a low-ball appraisal? What do you do then? This list can go on and on. These what-ifs and one-offs are addressed and covered in what are known as **contingency clauses**.

A contingency clause is a contract provision in your **purchase sales agreement** (PSA) that requires a specific event or action to take place for the contract to be considered valid. You can consider your contingency clauses as a form of protection to retrieve your **earnest money deposit** (EMD) in the event closing does not occur for a reason outside of your control.

While **contingency clauses** can help you with any unforeseen circumstances, in a competitive market, they can also hinder your chances of getting an approved purchase and sale agreement. You will want to consult with your agent or broker on what clauses work best for them. Just know that there are many different types of contingency clauses that can be added to your **purchase and sale agreement (PSA).** Knowing that anything is possible, let's just focus on some of the **most common contingencies** that come up:

Financial Contingency – If your offer is not a cash purchase, you will need to make sure your offer is contingent on obtaining financing with a not-to-exceed interest rate clause. This way, you will cover yourself in the event you cannot obtain financing or interest rates spike, affecting your ability to make monthly payments.

Appraisal Contingency – Under an appraisal contingency clause, if the home appraises for a significantly lower price than the contract value, the buyer can ask the seller to adjust the sales price so that it aligns with the appraised value or have the option to terminate the purchase and sale agreement with a full refund of the earnest money deposit (EMD).

If the property that you are interested in is part of a **homeowner's association (H.O.A.)** or **condominium association,** make sure your contract is contingent on your receiving the relevant documents with enough time to review them thoroughly. Make sure to sit down with your agent or broker and review the **(H.O.A.)** documents to make sure there are no additional costs or restrictions on your future home. You will want to go over the **Covenants, conditions,** and **restrictions (CC&Rs).** It is imperative that you understand all of the covenants, conditions, and restrictions before signing any contracts regarding the property you are interested in. 25% of new property owners get burned on this one. Make sure you disclose and discuss anything and everything you have plans for your new property.

Know that if a property was constructed before 1978, there may be a chance it contains **lead-based paint**, which could be harmful to inhale. According to the Centers for Disease Control, lead-based paint and lead-contaminated dust are the most widespread and hazardous sources of lead exposure.

Conducting a lead paint inspection will tell you the lead content of every painted structural fixture of your home. (Walls, doors, ceilings, windows, etc.) Nevertheless, it won't tell you whether the paint is a hazard or how you should deal with it. A risk assessment tells you if there are any severe lead hazards, such as peeling paint and lead dust, and what actions to take to address these hazards. Homes built after 1978 don't necessarily have this issue, so a lead-based paint contingency may not be required in that situation.

I know I have shared quite a bit of information. Therefore, it is imperative that you work with a good real estate agent or broker to help walk you through all that I have shared with you thus far.

You will want to get a **property condition report (PCR)** conducted. A certified inspector should conduct a property condition inspection that will give valuable perception of the condition of the property, with critical information such as the remaining life span of existing utilities, roofs, and appliances.

A certified inspector can find termites, safety hazards, water damage, broken appliances, etc. This inspection can save you thousands of dollars in costly repairs. In many cases, sellers are willing to fix these issues presented in the **Property Condition Report (PCR)** or credit you for the damages at settlement.

From my personal experience, the Property Condition Report (PCR) has either saved the buyer from purchasing a bad property or saved the buyer thousands of dollars in repairs. Make sure you work with a certified inspector who has the experience you need to deliver an adequate inspection that you can live with. And know that **cheaper is not always better, and better is not always cheaper**.

I am going to bring up this fact once again. **A <u>property appraisal</u> and a <u>property inspection</u> <u>ARE</u> <u>NOT</u> one in the same.** They are completely different and should be treated as such.

If this is not the first home that you will be buying and you need to sell your current home to buy this property, you will want to make sure your purchase and sales agreement (**PSA**) is contingent on the sale of your current home. You don't want to lose your **earnest money deposit** (**EMD**) in the event your current home does not sell.

A homebuyer can void a purchase contract if a title company reveals an issue that could prevent the buyer from becoming the property's new owner or any findings that affect the property's marketability or use.

A **pest control inspector** can generate a report identifying any potential termites or other insects that could be harmful to the property. Depending on your contingency clause, if any severe infestations are found, the seller will have the option to remedy the situation, offer you a credit for the necessary repairs, or you will be able to get a refund of your deposit and walk away from the purchase and sales agreement (PSA).

Next, you will want to submit your offer to the seller. You will want to draft a personal letter to the seller, along with the purchase and sales agreement (PSA). The personal letter can open doors that would otherwise be closed to the buyer. The personal letter will provide the seller with insight and create a personal connection to help your offer stand out.

With your offer, make sure also to provide the following documents:

- ✓ Have on hand **the preapproval letter** from your lender. Just keep in mind that the preapproval letter mentioned earlier in this book comes from your chosen lender and serves as proof that you qualify for financing up to a certain sum. It will normally be issued after a lender has had the chance to properly analyze your financial background. This letter will guide you to homes within your price range while offering you peace of mind that you can afford the homes you are looking at.

- ✓ You will want a copy of the **earnest money deposit (EMD)** check. Your agent or broker should be able to help you determine a deposit that shows you are serious. As I mentioned before, based on the housing market, this could be anywhere from $1,000 to 5% of the purchase price.

- ✓ **Once you have submitted an offer on the home in question,** the seller has two choices. Either they will accept your offer or counter with changes to terms or price. Online research shows that just under half of buyers have their first offer accepted.

According to online reports, 25% of buyers make two offers, and 20% make three or more offers until they agree to terms. If the seller counters you once again, you will be able to review the terms, conditions, and sales price with your agent or broker to help you make an informed decision. If the new terms, conditions, and sales price work for you, then fantastic. You can accept their offer. If the terms, conditions, and price give you a bad taste in your mouth, it will be up to you to counter again until terms, conditions, and price are agreed upon. Once the terms of the purchase and sales agreement (PSA) are accepted and signed by both the buyer and seller, the purchase and sales agreement (PSA) is considered ratified, and you are officially under contract.

CHAPTER TEN
AFTER SIGNING THE RATIFIED CONTRACT

Don't confuse needless activity with accomplishment.
-Dr. Mark L. Huddleston Ph.D.

Y ou are much closer to settling into your new home. You have made an informed offer and now have a **ratified purchase and sale agreement (PSA)**. The time frame between a ratified purchase and sales agreement and closing is when you are able to conduct inspections and appraisals and make sure the property is in good standing. From this point on, you will typically have 30 to 45 days, as outlined in your purchase and sale agreement (PSA), to fulfill your purchase contract.

✓ It is **time to pull out your calendar** and **make a list of all the key dates** set in the purchase and sale agreement (PSA) so you don't overlook and miss anything. You will want to take into consideration your contingencies along with their deadline dates, which depend on the allotted time frame specified in your contract. Using a calendar or personal planner can be a very helpful way to stay on top of important deadlines and keep yourself organized.

✓ At this time, you will want to **deposit your earnest money deposit** (EMD). You should mail out a copy of the ratified purchase and sale agreement (PSA) to your title company as soon as possible. Your earnest money deposit (EMD) proves to the seller that you will carry out the transaction in good faith. Know that failure to deliver the earnest money deposit (EMD) within the time frame allotted in the purchase and sale agreement (PSA) may result in a breach of the purchase and sale agreement (PSA) and nullify the agreement.

✓ **You will want to communicate with your lender right away** and send them a copy of the ratified purchase and sale agreement (PSA) and ask them what documents they need to get you approved and cleared to close. You must be proactive and make sure to provide this information to your lender in a timely manner. Here is a list of documents that your lender may request of you:

- Driver's licenses.
- Bank statements.
- 2 months of recent bank statements.
- Payments of utility bills.
- Tax returns from the last three years.
- Verification of funds.
- W2.

Keep in mind that this list may not be all that the lender will request of you. It is imperative to ask your lender for any additional information that you might need to gather for them.

In some cases, **your lender may give you the option of paying a fee to buy down your interest rate or locking your interest rate sixty to ninety days before closing**. This may be a good option depending on the market. You may want to sit with a financial advisor to get more information before proceeding. If all things are the same, I would recommend you use those funds to pay down your mortgage, which will effectively lower your monthly payment.

Once your loan is approved, your lender will provide you with a **closing disclosure (CD)**. A closing disclosure (CD) is a document that includes all the borrower's closing costs, as well as loan terms and monthly payments. Regulations require a lender to provide a mortgage borrower with the closing disclosure three business days before the loan closing.

✓ Next, **you will want to schedule inspections and appraisals.** You don't want to drop the ball when it comes to doing this. If your offer is contingent on any inspections or appraisals, you will want to schedule them as soon as possible. Inspectors and appraisers may need some lead time to coordinate with their schedules before the deadline. Your lender will probably want to have a report from an approved appraiser in hand before accepting your loan. This is why it is so important to coordinate with your lender as well.

Once your property inspector begins their duties, they will analyze and investigate the entire property from bottom to top. A certified inspector will be available to point out any of the major sewage, electrical, or other systems that may need to be addressed. The inspector will take note of where any problem areas are located and what needs to be fixed or examined.

Inspectors also identify issues that stand out or may require long-term maintenance. Generally, the inspection's purpose is to ensure there are no safety issues or costly repairs associated with the home that you did not know about.

Also, getting your **property inspected** will help you become more acquainted with the new home, better understand its components, and avoid potential concerns. While the inspector is a professional and will go over all items in detail, here are a few items you may want to check out for yourself and ensure they are inspected:

✓ From experience, I **have an inspector start with the electrical outlets** throughout the home. Some inspectors disregard electrical outlets. I will make sure that the inspector I have chosen will take the time to check each outlet to see that each outlet is working properly. Making sure all outlets are working can save you hundreds or even thousands of dollars in the long run.

✓ **Make sure that the inspector checks the heating, ventilation, and air conditioning (HVAC) units,** for they can be quite costly to replace. Costs could escalate to thousands of dollars, depending on the unit. You will want the inspector to check the condition as well as the expected remaining life of the unit.

✓ **Next, you will want to flush each toilet in the home** just to make sure they all are functioning correctly. You will not want to find out that one of your toilets is leaking or not flushing correctly after closing.

✓ **Make sure you have adequate water pressure and that you have both hot and cold water available for each sink, faucet, and shower.** If you find a problem with any of them, you will want to have the seller fix them or issue a credit at closing.

✓ **You will want the inspector to check the water heater** to ensure that it is working properly. Knowing the remaining life of the unit is a plus as well.

✓ Be mindful of completing a visual inspection to **look for water damage** to the baseboards, ceilings, and floors.

✓ Now, **if you live in a flood zone, I recommend that you purchase a sump pump**. Sump pumps are convenient features for pumping out any standing water that may gather under the house. I don't recommend that you buy a house that is in a flood zone, but the choice would be up to you. When purchasing a sump pump, you will want to make sure that it is fully functional. A faulty sump pump can cause a lot of extensive damage by backing up or pumping the water somewhere it shouldn't be going.

✓ Make sure you check **all windows in the household**. You will want to open and close every window in the home to confirm that the latches and locks are working as they should.

✓ When it comes to home appliances, **make sure the home inspector runs the dishwasher, stove, microwave, etc.**, to make sure they are in excellent working order. It is imperative that you check all hoses in the dishwasher, for they can become hard and brittle. Trust me when I tell you that you do not want a dishwasher to leak all over your home.

✓ **You will want to turn all lights off and on to make sure they work.** If there are any light bulbs that are out, you can ask the seller to replace them or ask the seller to replace them to match the other light bulbs in the fixture or room.

✓ Make sure that you **check all smoke and carbon monoxide detectors** throughout the home. You will want to see to it that they are functioning properly. Doing so could save your life and your home from a disastrous event. If smoke and carbon monoxide detectors are not working properly at the time of sale, most insurance companies may try to avoid paying deductibles in the event of a disaster.

The home inspector you have chosen will document all their findings and send them to you in an all-encompassing report. After your home inspector has certified that there are no significant issues and the deal is done, you will want to keep in mind where everything in the home is and start to make plans for both short-term and long-term maintenance projects.

Let's make sure that you understand the difference between a **property appraisal** and a **property inspection**. Appraisers estimate the value of a property and are normally called in to appraise the home before the final sale of the home. The appraiser will analyze the property and compare it to similar homes in the immediate area. Appraisers will note the unique attributes of both the property and the surrounding areas.

For instance, an appraiser may take note of a busy highway nearby, the condition of the roof and foundation, or the main integrity of the main dwelling. Appraisers will photograph the building's exterior as well as the interior of the home in order to document the condition of the property. Afterward, the appraiser will carefully consider the data to provide you with an accurate justification of the home's market value based on the home's condition and market equivalents.

Once you have received the appraisal and property condition report (PCR) back from the appraiser and inspector, you will have the opportunity to negotiate any potential repairs with the seller. Many sellers are willing to cover the repairs, while others may issue (credit) for any findings the inspector comes across.

At this point, it is time to consult with your agent or broker. You will need to consider the number of required repairs and the costs associated with reaching a reasonable conclusion with the seller. Ask your agent or broker for their opinion on this matter. Once again, it is imperative that your agent or broker earn their commission. They should be familiar with these different scenarios and be able to help you close these types of transactions.

Next, you will want to acquire home insurance. You will not want to get any type of insurance. You will want to get the correct insurance and coverage needed to protect your home. You will not want to go the cheap route. Ask your agent or broker for the name of a reputable home insurance agent and have them help you find the best rate and coverage plan for your home. You will want to consider your home's specific needs. Your insurance should start the day you close.

Mortgage lenders usually require each buyer to procure home insurance to secure the buyer's purchase. Know that many home insurance policies can be combined with your monthly mortgage payment and real estate taxes to create a single payment due monthly. Some insurance policies might need to be paid for separately, so check with the insurance agent you go with to see if there are any options, they can offer you for your specific situation.

Homeowners can select home insurance policies that fit their budget. One way of reducing or increasing the cost of your home insurance is by adding a deductible. A higher deductible will typically result in a lower-cost insurance plan. Nevertheless, you will want to be aware of weighing the pros and cons before you choose to add a deductible. You will want to think in case of an emergency. Deductibles will require the homeowner to come up with out-of-pocket costs. You will want to be conservative in selecting a deductible that fits your budget and addresses all of your homeowner needs.

I want to share a story of what happened to me when I bought my first home. The homeowner insurance agent had asked me what was the amount of my personal property that would occupy my home. I was about to inform the homeowner's insurance agent that the amount to replace all my personal belongings was only $30,000. My broker pulled me aside and told me that I had much more personal belongings than $30,000. You will not want to make this mistake. Two years after buying my home, someone broke in and stole most of my personal belongings, and it came out to $80,000 to replace all of my belongings that were stolen. Thank God, my broker pulled me aside and instructed me to increase my personal property amount. In the end, all of my personal belongings were replaced.

Know that a homeowner insurance policy usually does not cover earthquake or flood damage. If you live in an area prone to these natural disasters, I recommend that you include earthquake and flood add-on insurance in your homeowner policy. If your home is located on a fault line or your home is in a flood zone area, it is imperative that you get these insurances added on. Earthquake and flood damage can be extensive.

Furthermore, the Insurance Information Institute warns that disasters such as floods, earthquakes, and hail may require different deductibles. Be very clear about what is and isn't covered in your home insurance policy so there are no surprises later down the road.

Next, you will want to **make sure to turn on all utilities throughout the household**. You might not believe what I am about to share with you, but many times the new homeowner forgets to transfer the utilities into their name. With all the other things the new homeowner is inundated with, many times, this one is forgotten. You will want to make sure to call the appropriate utility companies before closing and have them **register the utilities under your name** as of the day of closing.

You will want to notify and update the homeowner's association (HOA). Make sure they have your contact information on file, along with the closing date. This will ensure that you receive correspondence, bills, and other notices.

If there are any contractors providing services for your property, make sure they are also aware of your new ownership start date and inform them of any services you may not want to continue.

Here are a few examples of some service contractors that may need contacting:

- ✓ Landscaping contractors.
- ✓ Pest control companies.
- ✓ Home Security Monitoring.
- ✓ If you have a pool (swimming pool maintenance companies).
- ✓ Newspaper delivery.

If you have done your due diligence and are comfortable with the property inspection report, your appraisal report came in at the same price or higher than your purchase price, you have secured your home loan and all contingencies have been waived, then you can move forward with closing. I would suggest submitting an addendum to the purchase and sale agreement removing all contingencies and stating that you are moving forward with the purchase of your new home.

CHAPTER ELEVEN
TIME TO CLOSE THE TRANSACTION

Our choices create our character,
and our character dictates our choices.
-Dr. Mark L. Huddleston Ph.D.

You are almost at the finish line. Closing is the process of finalizing the sale, signing the last set of documents, and transferring the remainder of the funds to the seller. The closing process is complete when the deed to the home is recorded. As soon as the deed is recorded, the home is officially yours.

I know what you're thinking. Will I have to do all of this by myself? The answer to that question is no! Closing is not handled directly by the buyer and seller but by a neutral agent. Often, closing is done by a title company that the buyer and seller have agreed upon in advance. You will also have your agent or broker there with you to answer any questions you should have.

Most title companies will also handle the escrow, and in other cases, a real estate attorney will handle this transaction.

There are several prerequisites to closing a property sale, and the closing agent's job is to ensure all are executed properly.

Here are the three most important requirements for closing a home sale:

- ✓ The buyer signs the deed of trust for the mortgage (if applicable).
- ✓ Your loan provider or your funds are transferred to the seller.
- ✓ The title to the property is transferred from the seller to the buyer.

Bear in mind that the sale proceeds are not the only item of monetary value exchanged during closing. Depending on how the sales contract was structured, there will probably be other fees that will have to be addressed, such as property taxes, agent or broker commissions, or title insurance. By being the buyer, you must complete four key steps for the property sale to close. Here they are:

First Step: You will have the option to complete a **final walk-through of the property** in question before the sale closes. I recommend that you exercise the walk-through option. This is typically done within twenty-four hours of the scheduled closing time. You just want to make sure that the home meets your expectations and that everything matches what was agreed upon in the purchase and sale agreement. You may think that all people are honest, but let me be the first to tell you that they're not.

Let me share a story with you about a scenario that happened to a client of mine. They had worked out an agreement that all the appliances were to stay in the home, along with the light fixtures. When my client conducted the final walk-through of the property a day before closing, they noticed that all of the appliances and light fixtures had been removed. My client was instructed to contact the closing agent to inform them of what had happened. The closing agent contacted the seller and ordered them to replace the appliances and light fixtures that were agreed upon in the purchase and sale agreement. The closing agent warned the seller that if they were not compliant with their request, the purchase and sale agreement would be disbanded. The lesson here would be not to let your guard down anytime during the home-buying process. It is better to be safe than sorry.

The final walk-through will be your opportunity to ensure that any repairs you have requested were completed and that any appliances or furniture that were supposed to be included are still there. Once the sale closes, you won't be able to request any of these items from the seller. So, it is very important that you are sure everything is as it should be during this step.

If something is missing or some of the repairs were not completed, don't worry; the escrow agent can hold an adequate amount of money in escrow to ensure the items are repaired after closing.

Second Step: You will want to decide how to take title to the property in question. Defining the type of title you are acquiring is very important. It determines the legal status of your ownership. How you take title to the property can have major consequences later that will affect how the property can be transferred, what happens to the property if you or a co-owner pass away, or how the property might be passed down.

Depending on what state you live in, there may be specific laws restricting how you can hold the title, and in some states, there are laws that can change the title depending on what you do after you've taken ownership.

Different states also have different laws regulating how property is taxed, which can vary based on how it is titled. I recommend that you consult with an attorney, agent, or broker so that you can make an informed decision on how your title choice will affect your property. To help you get an **understanding of the different types of titles**, here are a few examples I will share with you:

The most common form of tenancy for married couples would be "**Joint Tenancy with Right of Survivorship**". In most states, the title will default to this form of tenancy if the purchasers of the property are married. Joint tenancy conveys an equal interest in a piece of real property to each of the parties involved in the purchase of the property. The distinguishing factor of joint tenancy with the right of survivorship is that if one party passes away, the title transfers to the survivor in equal proportion. This rule applies whether or not the decedent has a valid will and overrides any contrary provisions that may be in the decedent's will. Joint tenancy requires four "unities" under the law:

- ✓ Title, which means each party must acquire title in the same deed or other title documents.
- ✓ Time which means each party must acquire the title simultaneously.
- ✓ Interest which means each party enjoys the same, equal share of ownership.
- ✓ Possession, which means each party enjoys the same right of use or possession of the property.

If one of the joint tenants sells or otherwise transfers their interest to an individual who was not part of the original joint tenancy, this dissolves the joint tenancy and automatically creates a "tenancy in common". In some states, you may find that joint tenancy is referred to as "tenancy by the entirety." In practice, this is the same as joint tenancy, but the owners must be married. In joint tenancy, there is no such requirement.

Next, I will cover **Tenancy in Common**. Just think of tenancy in common as a different version of joint tenancy. Tenants in common share equal rights to use and possession of the property and are not allowed to exclude any of the other tenants in common from using or possessing it. Nonetheless, this does not mean they have to pay for the property equally or own equal shares of the property. Accountability for costs like property taxes or repairs is proportional to the ownership share of the property.

If you hold **Sole Title or Fee Simple Absolute Title**, that means you, and you alone, are the owner of the property. This gives you complete power, privileges, and liabilities available to a property owner under the law. If you are married but have decided to claim the sole title, the deed will display this. For example, the deed may state Jane Lane, a married woman, takes possession as her sole and separate property.

You must be knowledgeable of where you live. In some states, like California, your titling may not be permanent. California is a community property state. In community property states, the law stipulates that if an individual takes sole title but uses a bank shared with a spouse to pay the mortgage and other property expenses, then over time, the law will recognize the title as a joint tenancy instead of sole title. I recommend that you consult with a real estate attorney regarding the specifics of your property and state laws. You will not want to gloss over this when closing on your property. I have seen this come back and haunt a person until their last days.

If you have a business, you will want to know about **partnerships, corporations, and trusts** and how they can affect you. It is important to know that titles can be vested in a partnership, corporation, or trust and do not have to be vested in an individual. Since the law recognizes partnerships, corporations, and trusts as legal entities distinct from the individuals that comprise them, partnerships, corporations, and trusts can have special tax and probate consequences or benefits.

Know that every state has its own laws and statutes. According to California probate law, trusts often supersede a will if a person has created both instruments. Meaning trusts can serve the same function as a will after death. I recommend that you consult with a licensed real estate or estate planning attorney if this is something you are interested in doing.

Furthermore, selecting how you want to acquire the title, it is essential to confirm that your title is protected. Title insurance safeguards home buyers and mortgage lenders against deficiencies or other issues regarding the title of property when there is a transfer of property ownership. If a title dispute surfaces during a sale, the title insurance company may be responsible for paying specific legal damages. It depends on the policy you go with. As always, I recommend that you get a title insurance policy. It is a one-time cost that helps prevent any potential issues later in the future.

I know that I have gone over many things thus far. I also know that some things may be redundant, **but how many times did your parents tell you to clean your room and you didn't.**

I want to make sure that you acquire your home without any trouble or snags.

Behold, you are now at the point you have always dreamed of. The **signing of the closing documents**. When signing the closing documents, reading the small print is vital. You will be presented with long-drawn-out documents full of legal jargon, so you may want to bring your agent, broker, or attorney to the signing to verify you understand all the closing documents and their potential implications. You will want to read everything so you are aware of what you are agreeing to and have your agent, broker, or attorney double-check to catch any errors before the closing documents are finalized.

This is not the time to be shy. If you have any questions or concerns about what you are signing, it is best you speak up immediately. There is no such thing as a stupid question, but the question not asked. It is better to be clear about something than to leave it to chance.

The **most important document in the closing package will be the settlement statement**. In some cases, referred to as the HUD-1. You should receive this document, usually labeled "estimated," at least one day before the scheduled closing date. With any luck, you have received preliminary settlement statements earlier for your review, so there are no surprises during closing.

The settlement statement is like an accounting ledger entry that breaks down all the costs concerning the real estate transaction. Like, your down payment, funds from your mortgage lender and any credits you may have received from the seller, and other expenses like closing costs, property taxes, realtor, and broker commissions that will go in and out of escrow. It will also specify the type of loan and loan number if any, the title/

escrow company's file number for this transaction, and the date and location of the settlement.

On the settlement statement, there will be two columns, one for the seller's debits and credits and one for the buyer's debits and credits. Reading this ledger of income and expenses will help you validate that nothing got left out or double charged.

At the bottom of the settlement statement, there will be two key line items for you to pay attention to:

Gross amount due from the borrower or buyer. The gross amount due from the borrower or buyer is the total amount with all closing costs and fees paid by you, the buyer, for the purchase of the home. This will include your initial deposit, down payment, and the principal amount of your mortgage (if applicable). This is the amount you will need to pay into escrow for the sale to close.

Gross Amount Due to Seller. This is the amount that the seller walks away with once the sale has closed. This amount should equal the sale price minus any existing loans the seller may have (which are usually paid out of escrow) and any settlement charges.

The following is a list of some potential charges you may see on your settlement statement:

Attorney Fees – If you have not paid your real estate attorney outside of the settlement, you could see their fee on the settlement statement.

Appraisal Fee – As I mentioned earlier in this book, your lender will ask that you get a certified appraiser to appraise the home of interest. Most appraisers require you to pay them upfront before they share the appraisal outcome with you. If you did not pay for this outside of closing, then it will appear on the settlement statement.

Home Inspection Fee – Most inspectors require you to pay a home inspection fee before they share their final report. If you did not pay this expense outside of closing, then you will find it on your settlement statement.

Document Fees – There will be a cost for the title company to prepare all the documentation that you will be signing.

Filing Fees – The cost to file and record your documentation with the city or county.

Escrow Fees – The cost for the title company, attorney, or escrow agent who is managing the closing on your accord.

Escrow For Miscellaneous Costs – Escrow will cover any outstanding miscellaneous costs to be handled outside of closing. These could be items not resolved from the home inspection, utility bills, or other additional charges.

Title Insurance – The cost of the title insurance policy is a one-time payment and covers you as long as you own the home.

Homeowners Insurance – The lender will require you to either pay the first year's insurance upfront or set aside the money for first-year payments in the escrow deposit account.

Homeowners Association (HOA) Setup Fee – If your home is part of an HOA or condominium association, you may be required to pay an initiation fee to get set up.

Final Step: You will want to transfer the remainder of your down payment to escrow. Once you are satisfied with the condition of your property and you have reviewed the settlement statement, it is time to spend some money. Your initial earnest money deposit (EMD) will be credited toward your down payment. Next, you will need to pay the remaining amount of your down payment or the entire purchase price if you are paying cash into escrow. If you are financing your purchase with a mortgage, your lender will coordinate with escrow separately to wire them the amount you are borrowing. Once you have completed all of these steps and the funds have been transferred through escrow, you have officially completed the purchase of your new property. WELL-DONE!!!

CHAPTER TWELVE
THINGS TO ADDRESS AFTER PURCHASING YOUR HOME

Too many people regard learning as an
event instead of a process.

- Dr. Mark L. Huddleston Ph.D.

Now that you have successfully purchased your home, there will be numerous responsibilities to take care of. I have compiled a list that will be divided up into three sections:

- ✓ Things you should have completed before closing.
- ✓ Things to complete in the first 30 days of homeownership.
- ✓ Long-term things to keep in mind for later in the future.

Once again, I do not want to come across as redundant about what I am sharing with you. I just want you to be happy and successful. I do not want you to suffer the pitfalls that are out there waiting for you if you don't dot your I's and cross your T's. Whatever you do, don't shortcut this process, or you will pay dearly later on down the line.

Important Things You Should Have Completed Before Closing

I Recommend: You Purchase A Home Warranty:
Even top home inspectors can overlook something. If you didn't buy your new home directly from a builder and a home warranty was not included in your purchase contract with the seller, you may want to consider purchasing a home warranty for at least the first year of new homeownership. Home warranties will protect you against any defects you uncover that were not revealed during the initial home inspection.

I Recommend: You Transfer All Utilities Into Your Name:
Please don't take this recommendation lightly. I have seen this happen over and over again. The buyer begins moving into their new home to find out that they do not have any water, gas, or electricity cut on. I repeat! Don't forget to transfer your utility accounts to your new address so you can start living in your new home without any trouble. For utilities, be sure to transfer the water, gas, and electrical utility services at your new home to your name or make appointments to have these utilities reactivated.

Things To Complete Immediately After Closing

I Recommend: You Make Sure Your Home Has Fire & Carbon Monoxide Alarms: Make sure all Fire & Carbon Monoxide Alarms have good power sources and are fully functional. In many cases, these alarms have been disconnected, or they are not functioning adequately. Never assume that these alarms are working. I recommend buying new alarms to make sure they are up to code.

I Recommend: You Get Fire Extinguishers For The Kitchen & Bedrooms: Fires can start at a moment's notice. You never know when you will need a fire extinguisher. I recommend Halon fire extinguishers. According to studies conducted by the National Fire Protection Association, cooking equipment is the leading cause of home fires and injuries. These fires are responsible for 49% of residential fires. Most fires that occur in the kitchen are grease fires, which can't be put out with water. It would be a good idea to keep a **halon** fire extinguisher near the kitchen. Doing this will safeguard your new home from this potential hazard.

I Recommend: You Change All Locks & Reprogram Garage Door Opener: You will want to change all locks on your new home. Changing your locks is like reassurance for you and your loved ones. The seller may be handing over the keys and the garage door opener, but there is no way to tell if someone else may have copies of those keys or one of the extra garage door openers. To ensure your privacy and security, you should have all exterior locks, doors, gates, and garage door openers rekeyed or reprogramed. A new lockset may cost you $75 to $150. It's just my opinion that you should go high-end when buying protection for your home. I am sure you would agree that cheaper is not always better, and better is not always cheaper. On average, many homes will have 2 to 3 exterior doors. This means that if you go high-end with the locks, it will cost anywhere from $300 to $450 and a little bit of time to change the locks and reprogram your garage door opener.

I recommend: You Get The Phone-Internet-Cable Turned On: Do not wait too late to get your phone, internet, and cable services turned on. Many times, a technician will have to come to your home to set up these services properly. Trust me when I tell you that you will want this taken care of before you move in. You will also want to have an idea of where you want these services located before the technician comes to your home.

I recommend: You Give Your Home A Thorough Cleaning Before Moving In: In many cases, it is standard practice to clean a home before selling it. In other cases, the seller does just enough to sell the home and nothing more. You can't be sure how thoroughly it was cleaned. To be sure that your home is thoroughly clean, you may want to personally clean it yourself or hire a professional cleaning service to complete this chore. The best time to have your home thoroughly cleaned would be before you move all your things into your new home. Whichever you choose to do will give you peace of mind that you will have a safe and sanitized home.

I recommend: You Update Your Address Information: When buying a home, there are many things that will have to be done, and one of those things will be updating your address information. You will want to keep a list of creditors, friends, and family members so that when you move, you can send them all your updated address information. You will want to do this right away, or your bills and personal correspondence will continue to go to your old address. Once again, it is imperative that you update your contact information to your new address with your state driver's license, post office, car registration, voter registration, etc.... and any important vendors you do business with, like the bank, credit cards, etc.... You can also forward any mail from your old address to your new home address by completing an online form on the United States Postal Services (USPS) website, USPS.com. Per their site, customers have three mail forwarding options:

Permanent Change of Address – A permanent change of address order provides for piece-by-piece forwarding of primarily First-Class Mail service for twelve months and periodicals for sixty days but generally does not provide the forwarding of USPS Marketing Mail service or package services. The customer's new address is provided to business mailers upon request through mailer endorsements on a mail-piece.

Temporary Change of Address – A temporary change of address order provides for piece-by-piece forwarding of primary First-Class Mail service and periodicals for a specified period but generally does not provide the forwarding of USPS Marketing Mail or package services mail.

Premium Forwarding Service Residential Service (PFS-Residential Service) – PFS-Residential service provides a single weekly shipment of all mail for a residence via Priority Mail service for a fee. The service can be extended for up to a year. PFS-Residential is temporary and is offered as an additional option to the free temporary or permanent change of address option.

I recommend: You Set Up Your Homeowners Association and Mortgage Installments Online: If you are a person who truly cares about your credit, you will not want to miss setting up your online installment payments for your HOA and

Mortgage accounts after closing your home purchase. You may not receive any information for a few weeks, but that doesn't mean you are not responsible for making payments on your accounts. I suggest that if you don't hear back from your HOA and/or Mortgage company right away, you should take it upon yourself to reach out to them so your first payment isn't late.

I recommend: You Go Over Your To-Do Check List Before Closing Out Your Escrow: This way, if you have any outstanding items that weren't resolved at closing, such as unpaid utility bills from the seller or any outstanding maintenance costs owed by the seller, you will want to be sure to follow up and resolve these outstanding issues by closing out your escrow.

Things To Complete Long Term

I recommend: You Conduct Preventive Maintenance Checkups On Your Home: Just like you go to the dentist or the doctor for yearly checkups, you will want to perform regular preventive maintenance on your home. Doing this can prevent larger problems from down the road. You will want to address seemingly minor issues immediately so they don't turn into expensive or potentially disastrous problems in the future. Here is a list of things that you will want to address on a timely basis:

I recommend: You Clean Out Your Downspouts And Winter-Proof Your Outside Water Lines: Don't think that this could ever happen to you. They have a saying that holds true. If it can happen, it will happen. No need to chance a downspout backup. In many cases, when downspouts back up, they can cause damage to the siding of your home or even cause leakage into the roof area. I have seen this many times. All of this could have been avoided by simply clearing out the downspouts once a year. You will also want to winter-proof your water lines. This is very important if you live in a cold climate. Water left in hose bibs or pipes can freeze and burst. We all know when water freezes it expands. This expansion can crack your pipes and create a devastating predicament. Each year, before the weather turns cold, you will want to find the shutoff valves for your hose bibs, which should be inside your house or in front of your house. Either way, you will want to remove any hoses from your outdoor spigots and drain them of any water before you store them. This happened to me in one of my summer homes. Let me tell you that it was a complete nightmare to correct the damage from the broken pipes due to freezing.

I recommend: You keep your heating, ventilation, and air conditioning unit in prime running shape. Your HVAC system has filters to remove dust and harmful particles from the air that get circulated throughout your home. You should change your filters to high-quality filters every 3 to 6 months. This will save you money on heating and cooling costs by keeping your HVAC systems running efficiently and will contribute to the unit's longevity as well. You may want to buy those filters in bulk, so you don't have to run to the store all the time to pick up some.

I recommend: You get a sump pump if your home is in a flood zone or beneath sea level. Sump pumps come in handy when water starts to gather around your home. Sump pumps can pump out any standing water that may pool under your home. If your sump pump is clogged or just not working properly, it could cause a lot of overwhelming damage by backing up or pumping the water somewhere it should not be going. If you have a sump pump, it is probably located in your basement or crawl space. Make sure to test your sump pump yearly to ensure that it is in excellent working order.

I recommend: You sit down with a tax attorney to **find out if you qualify for a government homestead exception**. This exception may or may not apply to you, but you will never know if it does if you never ask. You could be leaving money on the table at tax time for being lazy. Many counties have homestead exceptions that can provide property tax benefits for qualified applicants. These benefits work by reducing the assessed value of your home as recorded by your county tax collector and thereby reducing your property tax bill. Requirements vary from county to county, but most counties will give exceptions to veterans and senior citizens.

I recommend: **You execute a will or trust**. I know that most people don't want to think about their passing, but it is crucial that your most valuable asset is handled the way you want in a worst-case scenario. As mentioned earlier in this book, how your home is titled may be a major factor in what happens with your home after your passing. You will want to sit down with an attorney to learn what is the best way to prepare a will and/or trust. In many cases, if there is no will or trust at the time of passing, the estate goes into probate. In other words, your assets are up for grabs for anyone to obtain them. This happens more times than not.

I recommend: You **look into assigning a limited power of attorney**. Doing this will ensure that your home can be effectively managed, rented, or sold in case you are not able to do so for any reason. You will want to assign the limited power of attorney to someone you trust.

I recommend: You have an emergency plan in place. They say the best time to address an emergency is before it takes place. Constructing a comprehensive emergency plan in advance will save lives and save you financial headaches if anything were to happen. Here is a small list of items to add to your emergency plan. Know that you can add to this list. There is no one way of doing anything. What matters is having an emergency plan.

I recommend: You **create an emergency call list**. Make sure to create an emergency call list and keep it updated at all times. You will want to include a certified plumber, an electrician, your insurance agent, your HOA and condo association representative, and your utility providers, for starters.

I recommend: You **know where your electrical panel is and make sure you have labeled all circuit breakers** so you know the parts of the electrical system to which they correspond to.

I recommend: You **know where the main gas line shutoff valve is located and how it works**. Not many things are as dangerous as a gas leak in your home. It is vitally important to be able to shut off the gas in case of an emergency quickly. Most homeowners have no clue how to shut off the gas when it is important to do so. Don't be one of them!

I recommend: You **know where the main water shutoff valve is**. In the event of a serious leak or flood, being able to shut off the main water valve quickly will save you from costly or severe water damage.

I recommend: You **set a goal to pay off your mortgage as soon as possible.** Most people are under the misconception that once you close on your mortgage, you are the owner of the property. This would be the furthest thing from the truth. If you pay off the balance owed in full and have the deed of the property in hand showing you as the lien holder, that would be the only time you would be able to state that you are the true owner of the property. If the deed still shows the bank or loan originator as the lien holder, there is no way that you could consider yourself the owner of the property.

Now, if you took out a mortgage to buy your home, as most homeowners do, it's imperative that you have a plan of action in place to pay off your home as soon as possible. Some financial advisors will tell you to prioritize any extra income you have for retirement savings or for other types of investments before trying to pay off your home loan early. The choice is yours, so you should consider the other factors and how they will have an impact on your personal finances. Here is some food for thought. Only 65% of American homeowners own their homes. That is just a little over half of the American people. Only 44% of minorities own their home free and clear. That is nearly 29 percentage points lower than their white counterparts. Also, keep in mind that stock interest rates fluctuate all the time, whereas the interest rates on fixed mortgages stay the same throughout the life of the mortgage loan.

Paying off your mortgage in advance of the term noted offers guaranteed savings on interest costs. Keep in mind that tax laws can change, meaning you may not always be able to rely on the mortgage interest write-off.

Furthermore, there is an incalculable peace of mind knowing you own your home free and clear. Being debt-free while living in your home provides a lot of financial independence. When the economy is in a downturn, it can be comforting to know that the cost of the roof over your head is limited to property taxes and insurance without a monthly mortgage payment. It has been stated by some of the richest people in America that if you want to find financial freedom, you need to pay off all debt, and yes, that will include your mortgage.

Before constructing a sound plan to pay off your mortgage early, you will want to answer these next two questions honestly:

Do I have high-interest debt? – If you have credit card debt or student loans, those interest rates are likely higher than your mortgage. What this means is, you will be making more money if you pay off the high-interest debt first. Whatever interest rate you have, it might be a student loan with a 7% interest rate; if you pay off that loan, you would be making 7%. That's your immediate return, which is a lot safer than trying to pick a stock or trying to pick real estate, or whatever it may be.

Do I have enough excess funds to pay off my home early? – You will not want to empty your rainy-day cash fund just so you can pay off your mortgage. However, if you have enough extra money to save, put that money toward paying off your mortgage so you can own your greatest investment in full. Paying off your mortgage in full will allow you to begin accumulating wealth from that day on. Most people will never understand what I just shared with you. Their present philosophy will not allow them to. Only 5 out of 100 people will comprehend this concept. I truly hope you are one of the five.

The way to reach financial independence would be to create an emergency fund and pay off all of your outstanding debts, starting with the smaller ones and working your way up. You will achieve a great milestone by purchasing a home. You will want to remember to maintain your financial obligations and not neglect the smaller details when it comes to maintenance. This way, you will fully utilize your hard-earned investment, minimize any potential depreciation, and reap its full benefits.

CHAPTER THIRTEEN
HOME BUYING TIMEFRAME

> When you have a whole lot of people doing nothing,
> you have a whole lot of nothing getting done.
> *-Dr. Mark L. Huddleston Ph.D.*

A friend of mine once told me that real estate cannot be lost or stolen, nor can it be carried away. Purchased with common sense, paid for in full, and managed with reasonable care, it is about the safest investment in the world. I truly agree with this statement. The truth of the matter is that I did not always believe in these intensifying words. I was ignorant of the home-buying process. I was always told that the best time to buy a home was five years ago. Those words were from ignorant people who had no clue what they were talking about.

This will be a short chapter due to me already covering this information earlier in this book. Buying a home is a long-term commitment, and for that reason alone, most home buyers will want to take their time to make sure they are making an informed decision. According to a major real estate platform website, it takes an average of four and a half months to sign a purchase and sale agreement on a home. Furthermore, you can expect it to take one to two months to close on a home once under contract. Like anything else in the home-buying process, the timeline can vary dramatically, depending on your specific situation and market conditions. The following is a breakdown of how long each step in the home-buying process should take.

Preparing your finances can take up to six to nine months – If you are financially stable and have enough saved for a down payment, you may not need to prepare your finances. On the contrary, most home buyers will need to plan for this milestone. During the financial planning phase, you should:

- ✓ Talk to a certified financial planner and loan officer.
- ✓ Save as much as possible for your down payment or see if you can qualify for down payment assistance.
- ✓ Understand the costs associated with homeownership.
- ✓ Work on improving your credit score.
- ✓ Understand the various types of mortgages.
- ✓ Understand your financial situation by creating a budget and calculating your debt-to-income ratio.

Finding your home and making an offer can take anywhere from three to five months – According to a major real estate platform website research report, about 50% of home buyers search for a home for less than three months, 37% searched for less than six months, and 13% shopped for seven months to a year. During the period in which you're searching for a home and making an offer, you should:

✓ Interview real estate agents or brokers and sign an agency agreement.

✓ Search for properties online that fit your budget.

✓ Visit and tour properties in person.

✓ Understand market fundamentals, value, and home stats.

✓ Make an offer on a house that you feel comfortable calling home.

Signing post-ratified contracts can take anywhere from 30 to 45 days – There are many things that need to be addressed during a short time frame. The road to closing may be long and overwhelming. But it will be well worth it when everything is completed. During your study period, you should:

✓ You will want to stay in contact with your lender and provide the necessary documentation to get approved for your loan.

✓ Send a check to your escrow agent with your earnest money deposit.

✓ Schedule a home inspection and appraisal.

✓ Review the home inspection report and negotiate repairs or credits needed with the seller.

✓ Shop for homeowners' insurance.

✓ Waive any other contingencies in your purchase and sale agreement.

Closing can take anywhere from seven to ten days – Closing is a one-day occurrence, but preparing for closing can take anywhere from seven to ten days. To make it to closing, you will want to:

✓ Perform a final inspection of the property.
✓ Inform the title company of how you want to take title to your property.
✓ Review the settlement statement and closing documents.
✓ Wire the remaining balance owed.
✓ Get the keys to your new home.

CHAPTER FOURTEEN

Eleven Major Mistakes First-Time Buyers Make

Fools multiply when wise men and women stay quiet.
- Dr. Mark L. Huddleston Ph.D.

I have covered a lot of material in this book. I want to mention the eleven major mistakes that first-time home buyers make. I am sharing this information with you to prevent you from making the same mistakes that me and other investors have made over the years. At worst, these mistakes can cause problems later down the road when it comes time to sell.

Many real estate agents and brokers agreed that the average first-time buyer makes at least one of the following mistakes:

Mistake #1: Not checking out the homeowner's association CC&Rs before purchasing their home. I have seen this happen repeatedly. People purchase a home and come to find out that they can't do what they want to do with the property. For example, you find out that the homeowner's association won't allow you to rent the property you just bought, or you won't be allowed to put in a new bedroom or bathroom. You must find out the rules and regulations before even thinking about purchasing a home.

Mistake #2: Not timing your move correctly: As a first-time buyer, you may be renting or leasing at this present time. If so, the best time to close on a house is when your current lease ends. Don't sign another year-long lease if you expect to buy a home before that lease period expires; otherwise, you will end up making unnecessary penalty lease payments. Another option is to ask your landlord to include an escape clause in your new lease that will allow you to get out of your lease with thirty- or sixty days' notice.

Mistake #3: Looking at homes you can't afford: First-time buyers often listen to unqualified individuals stating that they can buy a home for up to two and a half times their combined income. But that's if interest rates are at 7 to 8 percent. If interest rates stay in the 4 percent range, you might be able to push that number to four times your combined income or more. Even with all that I have shared with you up until now, there are so many other costs you have to factor into the purchase, including the carrying costs on your debt, property taxes (paid once or twice annually or billed to you monthly along with your mortgage payment), private mortgage insurance (PMI) if you put down less than 20 percent, and the maintenance and upkeep on the property (if you buy a bigger, more expensive home it will simply cost more to maintain and keep up). Then there's this: If you look at homes you can't afford, you will get spoiled by how nice they are. When you finally come to your senses and start looking at homes in your price range, you will be disappointed by what you can comfortably afford. For example, if you have been looking at four-bedroom homes with attached garages in fine suburbs, a three-bedroom home is a so-so neighborhood with street parking is going to seem not nice enough for you. In order to save yourself the heartache, get prequalified or preapproved for your mortgage by a local lender. That way, you will know exactly how much house you can afford to buy.

Mistake #4: Buying The Wrong Size House: Many first-time buyers, especially those who are single and in their late twenties and early thirties, purchase one-bedroom condominiums. Why do they buy a one-bedroom? Usually, it is so much more affordable than a two-bedroom. What millennials don't realize is how likely it is that they will meet someone, fall madly in love, and marry. Unless you marry a next-door neighbor, who has a condo that can be combined with yours, that one-bedroom, one-bath condo will soon seem too small. For nearly the same price and possibly even the same location, your dollars might buy a two-bedroom, two-bath condo, which would give you some much-needed additional flexibility. (At the very least, it will give you the option to rent out the other bedroom for some extra income). When you buy property, you should think about how long you intend to live there. Will it be a five-year home? A ten-year home? Or will this home be the home you intend to die in? The average American family changes residences every five to seven years. If you are in your twenties, anticipate significant changes in your lifestyle within five to seven years. Buy smarter by planning for those changes ahead of time.

Mistake #5: Buying The First House That You Come Across: Coming from a cramped, one-bedroom rental or coming from living in your parent's house, almost any home will look good. In a sellers' market, you might be tempted to make an offer on the first home you see. But that's rarely a good long-term move. It is my suggestion that you look at ten to fifteen homes or more (**in person, not online**) to see what's on the market within your spending range. Season your mind and eyes by inspecting different types of homes: condos, townhouses, duplexes, and single-family houses. See what type of home generates an internal response. You can possibly find out that it could be very different from what you are imagining is the right type of home to buy. When you have narrowed down your choices to three or four, visit them again. By this time, some form of objectivity should have returned, and you will be able to make a sensible choice. Know that spur-of-the-moment decisions often don't work out, and you could wind up paying dearly for your impulsiveness.

Mistake #6: Buying Property That Is Difficult To Resell: You may tell yourself that you don't mind that your home backs up to a main freeway, but you will when it comes time to sell your home. It is unlikely you will be able to easily convince another buyer just how quiet and peaceful life is there. When buying a home, try not to buy one that will be difficult to resell. Even though you think you will be there forever, you probably won't. Actually, I can virtually guarantee that you won't spend the rest of your life in your first home. Most first-time buyers sell their homes within five to seven years, and there is no reason to think you will be any different. Before buying a house, you will want to think very hard about how you would go about selling it. You will want to walk yourself through and point out all the negative points concerning the property. Then get your agent or broker involved with making your decision. Ask them how long it would take them to sell to resell the property. Know that homes that are difficult to resell tend to appreciate at a slower rate than homes without significant issues for buyers to overcome.

Mistake #7: Overextending Your Budget: More times than not, this scenario happens to first-time home buyers. Although the lender who prequalifies you for a loan may tell you that you are able to afford a $300,000 home, keep in mind that buying in that price range may stretch your budget beyond your comfort zone. To avoid feeling financially squeezed or losing ground financially, it is important to understand how you spend your money and where those extra dollars go at the end of the month. You may be comfortable spending 35 percent of your take-home pay on rent, or you may prefer to spend less. Either way, write down every amount that you spend for two months. Find out if you can live without buying your streaming movie service. You need to find out if you would feel uncomfortable knowing you can go out to dinner once a month. Or that you will have to eliminate your annual vacation or your child's music lessons. As a homeowner, you will have additional expenses beyond your mortgage payment. You must understand that there is maintenance and upkeep of a home, plus property taxes. If you live in a condo, you will have other assessments. Buying a less expensive home will give you greater peace of mind and allow for savings.

Mistake #8: Suffering From Indecisiveness: When searching for the right house, you should take all the time you need. Don't let your agent or broker bully you into making a decision before you are ready to do so. Ask to see five, ten, twenty, or fifty homes if you haven't found a home you like enough to bid on. Indecisiveness kicks in when you have found a home you would like to live in but you are afraid of making a commitment. First-time buyers often lose out on two or three homes because they can't bring themselves to make an offer on a home in time. In other cases, there might be two wonderful properties, and they face a tough choice. If you are afraid, admit that fear and conquer it by talking with your agent or broker. You are not the only first-time buyer who will have trouble making up their mind. Just know that if you snooze, in most cases, you will lose.

Mistake #9: Choosing The Wrong Mortgage: Many first-time buyers have heard from their parents that the only mortgage to get is a thirty-year fixed-interest rate loan. That is because the generation ahead of you didn't have the tailor-made financial options buyers have today. Consider choosing an adjustable-rate mortgage (ARM) to take advantage of super-low interest rates. (I am not a fan of an adjustable-rate mortgage) Your monthly mortgage payment can triple in one month. Most people in the United States cannot handle an increase like that in monthly mortgage payments. Nowadays, you have the option to choose a ten or fifteen-year fixed-interest-rate loan to maximize your mortgage interest deduction and save you hundreds of thousands of dollars in interest. Explore all your options. Have your lender show you on paper how much each option will cost and how they compare with one another.

Mistake #10: Underinsuring The Property: First-time buyers know they have to buy home insurance to cover their mortgage. Sometimes they forget to increase the coverage of that insurance as the neighborhood improves and the home appreciates in value. Sometimes they forget to insure the contents of the house. Think about how much it would cost you to replace your furniture, clothing, books, laptops, artwork, and pots and pans. Add up everything and then tack on the cost of rebuilding the home (a single-family or townhouse) if it were to burn to the ground. Then add on your mortgage, which would still have to be paid. That is how much insurance you should buy.

Mistake #11: Not Putting Terms or Agreements In Writing: Out of all eleven mistakes I have covered thus far, this mistake makes the hair on my back stand upright. A handshake is fine when it comes to friendships or business acquaintances, but it has no place when dealing with contractors, builders, or business dealings of any kind. When it comes to financing, building, or buying a home, make sure everything you do is in writing, including the contract and amendments; specifications regarding appliances, tile, carpet, and other upgrades; and any change orders. Once the contract is signed, you must obtain a copy of the contract. This way, all parties will have to live up to the terms of the contract. Make sure you understand the terms of the contract and what rights you and the other parties have with respect to the work, delivery date, terms, and payment. Too often, important details are left out of the contract, details that can cost you dearly at closing.

CHAPTER FIFTEEN

ACRONYM AND GLOSSARY LIST OF REAL ESTATE TERMS EVERY HOME BUYER SHOULD KNOW

It's what you learn after you think you know it all that counts.
-Dr. Mark L. Huddleston Ph.D.

Y ou will want to get familiar with real estate acronyms and verbiage. I feel this is one of the problems that buyers come across when purchasing a home. Most buyers do not understand the verbiage used when purchasing a home. This is one of the number one reasons for foreclosures. It is imperative that you understand these acronyms and real estate terms to become successful in purchasing your first home. Here is a short acronym list:

ACRONYMS

ARM: Adjustable-Rate Mortgage.
CD: Closing Disclosure.

CMA: Comparative Market Analysis.

DOM: Days on Market.

EMD: Earnest Money Deposit.

FHA Loan: Federal Housing Administration.

FRM: Fixed Rate Mortgage.

HOA: Homeowner's Association.

HVAC: Heating, Ventilation, and Air Conditioning.

PCR: Property Condition Report.

PITI: Principle, Interest, Taxes, and Insurance.

PMI: Primary Mortgage Insurance.

PSA: Purchase and Sale Agreement.

USDA Loan: A loan provided by the United States Department of Agriculture.

USPS: United States Postal Service.

VA Loan: A loan provided by the United States Department of Veterans Affairs.

GLOSSARY

Abstract – A summary of the public records affecting the title to a particular piece of land. An attorney or title insurance company officer creates the abstract of the title by examining all record instruments (documents) relating to a specific piece of property, such as easements, liens, mortgages, etc.

Acceleration Clause – A provision in a loan agreement that allows the lender to require the balance of the loan to become due immediately if mortgage payments are not made or there is a breach in your obligation under your mortgage or note.

Addendum – Any addition to, or modification of, a contract. Also called an amendment or rider.

Adjustable-Rate Mortgage (ARM) – A type of loan whose prevailing interest rate is tied to an economic index (like one-year Treasury bills or LIBOR, the London Interbank Offered Rate), which fluctuates with the market. There are various types of ARMs, including one-year ARMs, which adjust every year; three-year ARMs, in which the interest rate is fixed for three years and then varies each year thereafter; and five-year ARMs, in which the interest rate is fixed for five years and adjusts every year thereafter. When the loan adjusts, the lender tacks a margin onto the index rate to come up with your loan's new rate. ARMs are far riskier than fixed-rate mortgages, but their starting interest rates can be lower than fixed-rate mortgages. Word of caution. I have seen a buyer's interest rate triple in one month. I have also seen millions of people lose their homes due to this happening to them. But the choice is yours. If it looks too good to be real, it usually is.

Agency – A term used to describe the relationship between a seller, agent, or broker or a buyer, agent, or broker.

Agency Closing – The lender's use of the title company or other party to act on the lender's behalf for the purposes of closing on the purchase of a home or refinancing of a loan.

Agent – An individual who represents a buyer or seller in purchasing or selling a home. Licensed by the state, an agent must work for a broker or a brokerage firm.

Agreement of Sale – This document is also known as the contract of purchase, purchase agreement, purchase and sale agreement, or sales agreement. It is the agreement by which the seller agrees to sell you their property if you pay a certain price. It contains all the provisions and conditions for the purchase and sale and must be written and signed by both parties.

Amortization – A payment plan that enables the borrower to reduce their debt gradually through monthly payments of principal and interest. Amortization tables allow you to see exactly how much you would pay each month in interest and how much you would repay in principle (the amount you owe on the loan), depending on the amount of money borrowed at a specific interest rate.

Application – A series of documents you must fill out when you apply for a loan.

Application Fee – A one-time fee charged by the mortgage company for processing your application for a loan. Sometimes the application fee is applied toward certain costs, including the appraisal and credit report.

Appraisal–An estimate of the value of your home provided by a certified appraiser.

Articles of Agreement for Deed – A type of seller financing that allows the buyer to purchase the home in installments over a specified period. The seller keeps the legal title to the home until the loan is paid off. The buyer receives an interest in the property – called equitable title but does not own it. However, because the buyer is paying the real estate taxes and paying interest to the seller, the buyer receives the tax benefits of home ownership.

Assumption of Mortgage – If you assume a mortgage when you purchase a home, you undertake to fulfill the obligations of the existing loan agreement the seller made with the lender. The obligations are similar to those you would incur if you took out a new mortgage. When assuming a mortgage, you become personally liable for the payment of principal and interest. The seller, or original mortgagor, is released from the liability and should get that release in writing. Otherwise, they could be liable if you don't make the monthly payments.

Balloon Mortgage – A type of mortgage that is generally short in length but is amortized over twenty-five or thirty years so that the borrower pays a combination of interest and principal each month. At the end of the loan term, the entire balance of the loan must be repaid at once.

Broker – An individual who acts as the agent of the seller or buyer. A real estate broker must be licensed by the state.

Building Line or Setback – The distance from the front, back, or side of a lot beyond which construction or improvements may not extend without permission by the proper governmental authority. The building line may be established by a filed plat of subdivision, by restrictive covenants in deeds, by building codes, or by zoning ordinances.

Buy Down – An incentive a developer or seller offers that allows the buyer to lower their initial interest rate by putting up a certain amount of money. A buy-down also refers to the process of paying extra points up front at the closing of your loan in order to have a lower interest rate over the life of the loan.

Buyer's Broker – A buyer's broker is a real estate broker who specializes in representing buyers. Unlike a seller's broker or conventional broker, the buyer's broker has a fiduciary duty to the buyer because the buyer accepts the legal obligation of paying the broker. The buyer's broker is obligated to find the best property for a client and then negotiate the best possible purchase price and terms.

Buyer's Market – Market conditions that favor the buyer. A buyer's market is usually expressed when there are too many homes for sale, and a home can be bought for less money.

Capital Gains – Profit made from the sale of a property. You should sit down with a tax accountant when selling your property. I have seen many home-sellers suffer great penalties due to not knowing the tax implications that come with capital gains taxes.

Certificate Of Title – A document or instrument issued by a local government agency to a homeowner, naming the homeowner as the owner of a specific piece of property. At the sale of the property, the certificate of title is transferred to the buyer. The agency then issues a new certificate of title which is transferred to the buyer. The agency then issues a new certificate of title to the buyer.

Chain Of Title – The lineage of ownership of a particular property.

Closing – The day when buyers and sellers sign the papers and actually swap money for the title to the new home. The closing finalizes the agreements reached in the sales agreement. Also called the settlement.

Closing Costs – The expenses above the property price that buyers and sellers normally incur to complete a real estate transaction. This phrase can refer to a lender's costs for closing on a loan, or it can mean all the costs associated with closing on a piece of property. Considering all closing costs, it's easy to see that closing can be expensive for both buyers and sellers. A home buyer's closing costs might include lender's points, loan origination or loan service fees; loan application fee; lender's appraisal fee; prepaid interest on the loan; lender's insurance escrow; lender's real estate tax escrow; lender's tax escrow service fee; cost for the lender's title policy; special endorsements to the lender's title policy; house inspections fees; title company closing fee; a deed or mortgage recording fees; local municipal, county, and state taxes; and the attorney's fee. A seller's closing costs might include a survey (which in some parts of the country is paid by the buyer); title insurance; recorded release of the mortgage; broker's commission; state, county, and local municipality transfer taxes; credit to the buyer for unpaid real estate taxes and other bills; attorney's fees; FHA fees and costs.

Closing Disclosure – A form that provides final details on the closing costs and mortgage for your home. It includes loan terms, your projected monthly payments, and how much you will pay in fees and other costs to close on the property.

Cloud On Title – An outstanding claim or encumbrance that adversely affects the marketability of a property.

Commission – The amount of money paid to the agent or broker by the seller or buyer as compensation for selling the home. Usually, the commission is a percentage of the sales price of the home and generally hovers in the 5 to 7 percent range. There is no set commission rate. It is always and entirely negotiable.

Comparative Market Analysis – An estimate of a home's value based on recently sold, similar properties in the immediate area.

Condemnation – The government holds the right to condemn land for use, even against the will of the owner. The government, however, must pay a fair market price for the land. Condemnation may also mean that the government has decided that a particular piece of land, or a dwelling, is unsafe for human habitation.

Condominium – A dwelling of two or more units in which you individually own the interior space of your unit and jointly own common areas such as the lobby, roof, parking, plumbing, and recreational areas.

Contingency – A contingency clause defines a condition or action that must be met for a real estate contract to become binding.

Contract to purchase – Another name for agreement of sale.

Contractor – In the building industry, the contractor is the individual who contracts to build the property. They erect the structure and manage the subcontracting (the electrician, plumber, etc.). Until the project is completed.

Conventional Mortgage – A conventional mortgage means that banks, savings, and loans, or other types of mortgage companies underwrite the loan. There are also certain limitations imposed on conventional mortgages that allow them to be sold to private institutional investors (like pension funds) on the secondary market.

Co-op – Cooperative housing refers to a building, or a group of buildings, that a corporation owns. The shareholders of the corporation are the people who live in the building. They own the shares of the property, which gives them the right to lease a specific unit within the building. In the corporation that owns the building and pays rent or monthly maintenance assessments for the expenses associated with living in the building. Co-ops are relatively unknown outside of New York, Chicago, and a few other cities. Since the 1970s, condominiums have become more common.

Counteroffer – When the seller or buyer responds to a bid, if you decide to offer $200,000 for a home listed at $250,000, the seller might counter your offer and propose that you purchase the home for $240,000. That new proposal, and any subsequent offer, is called a counteroffer.

Covenant – Assurances or promises set out in the deed or a legally binding contract implied in the law. For example, when you obtain title to a property by warranty, this is the Covenant of Quiet Enjoyment, which gives you the right to enjoy your property without disturbances.

Credit Report – A lender will decide whether or not to give you a loan based on your credit history. A credit report lists all your credit accounts (such as charge cards and personal loans), and any debts or late payments that have been reported to the credit company.

Cul-de-sac – A street that ends in a U-shape, leading the driver or pedestrian back to the beginning. The cul-de-sac has become exceptionally popular with modern subdivision developers, who use the design technique to create quiet streets and gives the development a secluded country feel.

Custom Builder – A home builder who builds houses for individual owners' specifications. The home builder may either own a piece of property or build a home on someone else's land.

Debt Service – The total amount of debt (credit cards, personal loans, mortgages) that an individual is carrying at any one time.

Debt-To-Income Ratio (DTI) – A personal financial measurement that looks at your total debt compared to your overall income.

Declaration Of Restrictions – Developers of condominiums (or any other type of housing unit that functions as a condo) are required to file a condominium declaration, which sets out the rules and restrictions for the property, the division of ownership, and the rights and privileges of the owners. The "condo dec" or "homeowner's dec," as it is commonly called, reflects the developer's original intent and may only be changed by unit-owner vote. There are other types of declarations, including homeowners' association and townhouse association. A similar type of document governs co-op dwellers. Sometimes referred to as the CC&Rs.

Deed – The document used to transfer ownership of a property from seller to buyer.

Deed of Trust – A deed of trust or trust deed is an instrument similar to a mortgage that gives the lender the right to foreclose on the property if there is a default under the trust deed or note by the borrower.

Deposit – Money given by the buyer to the seller with a signed contract to purchase or offer to purchase as a show of good faith. Also called an (earnest payment).

Down Payment – The case put into a purchase by the borrower. Lenders like to see the borrower put at least 20 % down in cash because lenders generally believe that if you have a higher cash down payment, it is less likely that the home will go into foreclosure.

Dual Agency – When a real estate agent or broker represents both the buyer and the seller in a single transaction, it creates a situation known as dual agency. In most cases, the agent or broker must disclose to the buyer and to the seller whom they are representing. Even with disclosure, the dual agency presents a conflict of interest for the agent or broker in the transaction. If the agent or broker is acting as the seller's agent or broker and the subagent for the seller (by bringing the buyer), then anything the buyer tells the agent or broker must by law be brought to the seller's attention. If the agent or broker represents the seller as the seller's agent or broker and the buyer as a buyer's agent or broker in the same transaction, the agent or broker will receive money from both the buyer and the seller, an obvious conflict of interest.

Due On Sale Clause – Nearly every mortgage has this clause, which states that the mortgage must be paid off in full upon the sale of the home.

Duplex – A duplex is generally a property divided into two separate living units. Those units can be situated side by side or stacked one on top of the other. There are separate entrances for each unit, and sometimes there are separate garages and yards, as well.

Earnest Money Deposit – a deposit made to a seller that represents a buyer's good faith to buy a home.

Easement – A right given by a landowner to a third party to make use of the land in a specific way. There may be several easements on your property, including for the passage of utility poles and lines, sewer or water mains, and even a driveway. Once the right is given, it continues indefinitely or until released by the party who received it.

Eminent Domain – The right of the government to condemn private land for public use. The government must, however, pay full market value for the property.

Encroachment – When your neighbor builds a garage or a fence, and it occupies your land, it is said to "encroach on" your property.

Encumbrance – A claim or lien, or interest in a property by another party. An encumbrance hinders the seller's ability to pass good, marketable, and unencumbered title to you.

Escrow Closing – A third party, usually a title company, acts as the neutral party for the receipt of documents for the exchange of the deed by the sellers for the buyer's money. The final exchange is completed when the third party determines that certain preset requirements have been satisfied.

Escrow (for earnest money) – The document that creates the arrangement whereby a third party or broker holds the earnest money for the benefit of the buyer and seller.

Escrow (for real estate taxes and insurance) – An account in which monthly installments for real estate taxes and property insurance are held usually in the name of the home buyer's lender.

Fee Simple – The most basic type of ownership, under which the owner has the right to use and dispose of the property at will.

Fiduciary Duty – A relationship of trust between an agent or broker and a seller or a buyer's agent or broker and buyer, or an attorney and a client.

First Mortgage – A mortgage that takes priority over all other voluntary liens.

Fixture – Personal property, such as a built-in bookcase, furnace, hot water heater, or recessed lights, that become "affixed" because it has been permanently attached to the home.

Foreclosure – The legal action taken to extinguish a homeowner's rights and interest in a property so that the property can be sold in a foreclosure sale to satisfy a debt.

Gift Letter – A letter to the lender indicating that a gift of cash has been made to the buyer and that it is not expected to be repaid. The letter must detail the amount of the gift and the name of the giver.

Good Faith Estimate (GFE) – Under RESPA, lenders are required to give potential borrowers a written Good Faith Estimate of closing costs within three days of application submission.

Grace Period – The period of time after a loan payment due date in which a mortgage payment may be made and not be considered delinquent.

Graduated Payment Mortgage – A mortgage in which the payments increase over the life of the mortgage, allowing the borrower to make very low payments at the beginning of the loan. Also called an Option (ARM).

Hazard Insurance – Insurance that covers the property from damage that might materially affect its value. Also known as homeowners' insurance.

Holdback – An amount of money held back at closing by the lender or the escrow agent until a particular condition has been met. If the problem is a repair, the money is kept until the repair is made. If the repair is not made, the lender or escrow agent uses the money to make the repair. Buyers and sellers may also have holdbacks between them to ensure that specific conditions of the sale are met.

Home Inspection – The service an inspector performs when he or she is hired to scrutinize the home for any possible structural defects. It may also be done in order to check for the presence of toxic substances, such as lead paint or water, asbestos, radon, or pests, including termites.

Home Warranty – A service contract that covers the cost of maintaining household systems or appliances for a set period (typically one year).

Homeowner's Association (HOA) – An organization in a subdivision, planned community, or condominium building that makes and enforces rules for the properties and residents. Those who purchase property within an HOA's jurisdiction automatically become members and are required to pay dues, known as HOA fees.

Homeowner's Insurance – A form of property insurance that covers losses and damages to an individual's residence, including furnishings and other assets in the home.

Home Warranty – A service contract that covers appliances (with exclusions) in working conditions in the home for a certain period of time, usually one year. Homeowners are responsible for a per-call service fee. There is a homeowner's warranty for new construction. Some developers will purchase a warranty from a company specializing in new construction for the homes they sell. A homeowner's warranty will warrant the good working order of the appliances and workmanship of a new home for between one and ten years; for example, appliances might be covered for one year, while the roof may be covered for several years.

Housing and Urban Development Department – Also known as HUD, this is the federal department responsible for the nation's housing programs. It also regulates **RESPA**, The **Real Estate Settlement Procedures Act**, which governs how lenders must deal with their customers.

Loan – An amount of money that is lent to a borrower, who agrees to repay it plus interest.

Loan Commitment – A written document that states that a mortgage company has agreed to lend a buyer a certain amount of money at a certain rate of interest for a specific period of time, which may contain sets of conditions and a date by which the loan must close.

Loan Modification – A loan modification occurs when a mortgage lender agrees to modify the terms of an existing loan by changing the interest rate, length of the loan, or other payment terms. The loan modification is completed with a written document outlining the change in loan terms. Frequently, homeowners must apply to the lender for the loan modification.

Loan Origination Fee – A one-time fee charged by the mortgage company to arrange the financing for the loan.

Loan to Value Ratio – The ratio of the amount of money you wish to borrow compared to the value of the property you wish to purchase. Institutional investors (who buy loans on the secondary market from your mortgage company) set up certain ratios that guide lending practices. For example, the mortgage company might only lend you 80% of a property's value.

Location – Where property is geographically situated. "Location, location, location" is an agent or broker's maxim that states that where the property is located is its most important feature because you can change everything about a house except its location.

Lock-In – The mechanism by which a borrower locks in the interest rate that will be charged on a particular loan. Usually, the lock lasts for a certain time period, such as 30, 45, or 60 days. On new construction, the lock may be much longer.

Installment Contract – The purchase of property in installments. The title to the property is given to the purchaser when all installments are made.

Institutional Investors or Lenders – Private or public companies, corporations, or funds (such as pension funds) that purchase loans on the secondary market from commercial lenders such as banks and savings and loans. Or they are sources of funds for mortgages through mortgage brokers.

Interest – Money paid regularly at a particular rate for the use of borrowed funds from the lender.

Interest-Only Mortgage – A loan in which only the interest is paid on a regular basis (usually monthly), and the principal is owed in full at the end of the loan term.

Interest Rate Cap – The total number of percentage points that an adjustable-rate mortgage (ARM) might rise over the life of the loan.

Joint Tenancy – An equal, undivided ownership in a property taken by two or more owners. Under joint tenancy, there are rights of survivorship, which means that if one of the owners dies, the surviving owner, rather than the heirs of the estate, inherits the other's total interest in the property.

Landscape – The trees, flowers, planting, lawn, and shrubbery that surround the exterior of a dwelling.

Last Will and Testament – A legal document that communicates a person's final wishes pertaining to assets and dependents.

Late Charge – A penalty applied to a mortgage payment that arrives after the grace period (usually the 10th or 15th of a month).

Lease With An Option To Buy – When the renter or lessee of a piece of property has the right to purchase the property for a specific period at a specific price. Usually, a lease with an option to buy allows a first-time buyer to accumulate a down payment by applying a portion of the monthly rent toward the down payment.

Lender – A person, company, corporation, or entity that lends money for the purchase of real estate.

Letter of Intent–A formal statement, usually in letter form, from the buyer to the seller stating that the buyer intends to purchase a specific piece of property for a specific price on a specific date.

Leverage – Using a small amount of cash, say a 10 or 20 percent down payment, to purchase a piece of property.

Lien – An encumbrance against the property, which may be voluntary or involuntary. There are many kinds of liens, including a tax lien (for unpaid federal, state, or real estate taxes), a judgment lien (for monetary judgments by a court of law), a mortgage lien (when you take out a mortgage), and a mechanic's lien (for work done by a contractor on the property that has not been paid for). For a lien to be attached to the property's title, it must be filed or recorded with local county government.

Listing – A property that a broker agrees to list for sale in return for a commission.

Loan – An amount of money that is lent to a borrower, who agrees to repay it plus interest.

Loan Commitment – A written document that states that a mortgage company has agreed to lend a buyer a certain amount of money at a certain rate of interest for a specific period, which may contain sets of conditions and a date by which the loan must close.

Loan Modification – A loan modification occurs when a mortgage lender agrees to modify the terms of an existing loan by changing the interest rate, length of the loan, or other payment terms. The loan modification is completed with a written document outlining the change in loan terms. Frequently, homeowners must apply to the lender for the loan modification.

Loan Origination Fee – A one-time fee charged by the mortgage company to arrange the financing for the loan.

Maintenance Fee – The monthly or annual fee charged to condominium, co-op, or townhouse owners and paid to the homeowners' association for the maintenance of common property. Also called an assessment.

Mortgage – A debt instrument secured by the collateral of specified real estate property that the borrower is obliged to pay back with a predetermined set of payments.

Mortgage Banker – A company or corporation, like a bank, that lends its own funds to borrowers in addition to bringing together lenders and borrowers. A mortgage banker may also service the loan (like collecting the monthly payments).

Mortgage Broker – A company or individual that brings together lenders and borrowers and processes mortgage applications.

Mortgagee – A legal term for the lender.

Mortgagor – A legal term for the borrower.

Multiple Listing Service (MLS) – You are going to hear (MLS) quite a bit, so know what it means. It is a computerized listing of all properties offered for sale by member brokers. Buyers may only gain access to the (MLS) by working with a member broker.

Negative Amortization – A condition created when the monthly mortgage payment is less than the amount necessary to pay off the loan over the period of time set forth in the note. Because you're paying less than the amount necessary, the actual loan amount increases over time. That is how you end up with negative equity. To pay off the loan, a lump-sum payment must be made.

Opportunity Cost – The loss of potential gain from other alternatives when one alternative is chosen.

Option – When a buyer pays for the right or option to purchase property for a given length of time without having the obligation to purchase the property.

Origination Fee – A fee charged by the lender for allowing you to borrow money to purchase property. The fee that is also referred to as points is usually expressed as a percentage of the total loan amount.

Ownership – the absolute right to use, enjoy, and dispose of property. In other words, you own it!

Package Mortgage – A mortgage that uses both real and personal property to secure a loan.

Paper – Slang usage that refers to the mortgage, trust deed, installment, and land contract.

Personal Property – Moveable property, such as appliances, furniture, clothing, and artwork.

PITI – An acronym for **Principal, Interest, Taxes,** and **Insurance**. These usually make up your monthly mortgage payment.

Pledged Account – Borrowers who do not want to have a real estate tax or insurance escrow administered by the mortgage servicer can, in some circumstances, pledge a saving account with enough money to cover real estate taxes and the insurance premium must be deposited. You must then make the payments for your real estate taxes and insurance premiums from a separate account. If you fail to pay your taxes or premiums, the lender is allowed to use the funds in the pledged account to make those payments.

Point – A point is 1 percent of the loan amount.

Possession – Being in control of a piece of property and having the right to use it to the exclusion of all others.

Power of Attorney – A legal document giving authoritative power to someone to act on behalf of another person in specified legal or financial matters.

Prepaid Interest – Interest paid at closing for the number of days left in the month after closing. For example, if you close on the 15th, you would prepay the interest for the 16th through the end of the month.

Prepayment Penalty – a fine imposed when a loan is paid off before it comes due. Many states now have laws against prepayment penalties, although banks with federal charters are exempt from state laws. If possible, do not use a mortgage that has a prepayment penalty, or you will be charged a hefty fee in some cases if you sell your property before your mortgage has been paid off.

Prequalifying For A Loan – when a mortgage company tells a buyer in advance of the formal application approximately how much money the buyer can afford to borrow.

Principal – The original sum of money borrowed in a loan.

Private Mortgage Insurance (PMI) – Special insurance that specifically protects the top 20% of a loan, allowing the lender to lend more than 80% of the value of the property. PMI is paid in monthly installments by the borrower.

Property Condition Report – An evaluation of the current safety condition and capital expenses that will likely be required to maintain an asset in the short and long term.

Property Tax – A tax levied by a county or local authority on the value of real estate.

Proration – The proportional division of certain costs of home-ownership. Usually used at closing to figure out how much the buyer and seller each owe for certain expenditures, including real estate taxes, assessments, and water bills.

Purchase and Sale Agreement – A binding legal contract that obligates a buyer to buy and a seller to sell a property.

Purchase Money Mortgage – An instrument used in seller financing, a purchase money mortgage is signed by a buyer and given to the seller in exchange for a portion of the purchase price.

Quit-Claim Deed – A deed that operates to release any interest in a property that a person may have without a representation that they have a right in that property.

Real Estate – Land and anything permanently attached to it, such as buildings and improvements.

Real Estate Agent – An individual licensed by the state who acts on behalf of the seller or buyer. For their services, the agent receives a commission, which is usually expressed as a percentage of the sales price of a home and is split with their real estate firm. A real estate agent must either be a real estate broker or work for one.

Real Estate Attorney – An attorney who specializes in the purchase and sale of real estate.

Real Estate Broker – An individual who is licensed by the state to act as an agent on behalf of the seller or buyer. For their services, the broker receives a commission, which is usually expressed as a percentage of the sales price of a home.

Real Estate Settlement Procedures Act (RESPA) – This federal statute was originally passed in 1974 and contains provisions that govern the way companies involved with a real estate closing must treat each other and the consumer. For example, one section of RESPA requires lenders to give consumers a written Good Faith Estimate within three days of making an application for a loan. Another section of RESPA prohibits title companies from giving referral fees to brokers for steering business to them.

Realtist – A designation given to an agent or broker who is a member of the **National Association of Real Estate Brokers**.

Realtor – A designation given to a real estate agent or broker who is a member of the National Association of Realtors.

Recording – The process of filing documents at a specific government office. Upon such recording, the document becomes part of the public record.

Redlining – The slang term used to describe an illegal practice of discrimination against a particular racial group by real estate lenders. Redlining occurs when lenders decide certain areas of a community are too high risk and refuse to lend to buyers who want to purchase property in those areas, regardless of their qualifications or creditworthiness.

Regulation Z – Also known as the Truth in Lending Act. Congress determined that lenders must provide a written **Good Faith Estimate** of closing costs to all borrowers and provide them with other written information about the loan.

Reserve – The amount of money set aside by a condo, co-op, or homeowners' association for future capital improvements.

Sale-leaseback – A transaction in which the seller sells a property to a buyer, who then leases the property back to the seller. This is accomplished within the same transaction.

Sales Contract – The document by which a buyer contracts to purchase a property. Also known as the purchase contract or a contract to purchase.

Second Mortgage – A mortgage that is obtained after the primary mortgage and whose rights for repayment are secondary to the first mortgage.

Seller's Broker – A broker who has a fiduciary responsibility to the seller. Most brokers are seller's brokers, although an increasing number are buyer's brokers, who have a fiduciary responsibility to the buyer.

Settlement Date – The date when a trade is final, and the buyer must make payment to the seller while the seller delivers the property title.

Settlement Statement – A document that summarizes the terms and conditions of a settlement. It provides full disclosure of a loan's terms and conditions and all the fees and charges that a borrower must pay.

Shared Appreciation Mortgage – A relatively new mortgage used to help first-time buyers who might not qualify for conventional financing. In a shared appreciation mortgage, the lender offers a below-market interest rate in return for a portion of the profits made by the homeowner when the property is sold. Before entering into a shared appreciation mortgage, be sure to have your real estate attorney review the documentation.

Special Assessment – An additional charge levied by a condo or co-op board to pay for capital improvements or other unforeseen expenses.

Subagent – A broker who brings the buyer to the property. Although subagents would appear to be working for the buyer (a subagent usually ferries around the buyer, showing them properties), they are paid by the seller and have a fiduciary responsibility to the seller. Subagency is often confusing to first-time buyers, who think that because the subagent shows them property, the subagent is their agent rather than the seller's.

Subdivision – The division of a large piece of property into several smaller pieces. Usually, a developer or a group of developers will build single-family or duplex homes of a similar design and cost within one subdivision.

Tax Lien – A lien that is attached to property if the owner does not pay their real estate taxes or federal income taxes. If overdue property taxes are not paid, the owner's property might be sold at auction for the amount owed in back taxes.

Tenancy By The Entirety – A type of ownership whereby both the husband and wife own the complete property. Each spouse has an ownership interest in the property as their marital residence, and, as a result, creditors cannot force the sale of the home to pay back the debts of one spouse without the other spouse's consent. There are rights of survivorship whereby upon the death of one spouse, the other spouse would immediately inherit the entire property.

Tenants In Common – A type of ownership in which two or more parties have an undivided interest in the property. The owners may or may not have equal shares of ownership, and there are no rights of survivorship. However, each owner retains the right to sell their share in the property as they see fit.

Title – The legal ownership and legal right to use and enjoy a piece of property.

Title Company – The corporation or company that insures the status of title (title insurance) through the closing and may handle other aspects of the closing.

Title Insurance – Title insurance protects real estate owners and lenders against any property loss or damage they might experience because of liens, encumbrances, or defects in the title to the property.

Trust Account – An account used by brokers and escrow agents, in which funds for another individual are held separately, and not commingled with other funds.

Underwriter – One who underwrites a loan for another. Your lender will have an investor underwrite your loan.

Variable Interest Rate – An interest rate that rises and falls according to a particular economic indicator, such as Treasury Bills.

Void – A contract or document that is not enforceable.

Voluntary Lien – A lien, such as a mortgage, that a homeowner elects to grant to a lender.

Waiver – The surrender or relinquishment of a particular right, claim, or privilege.

Warranty – A legally binding promise given to the buyer at closing by the seller, generally regarding the condition of the home, property, or other matter.

Zoning – The right of the local municipal government to decide how different areas of the municipality will be used. Zoning ordinances are the laws that govern the use of the land.

NOW THAT YOU KNOW WHAT TO DO,

GO OUT AND DO IT!

Milton Keynes UK
Ingram Content Group UK Ltd.
UKHW020645201123
432908UK00019B/2524